Cheap AND *Easy!*

WHIRLPOOL WASHER REPAIR

7th EDITION

Written ESPECIALLY for Do-It-Yourselfers, Trade Schools, and other "green" technicians!

By Douglas Emley

Distributed exclusively by:

 EB Marketing Group

Lake Havasu City, AZ ● 800-400-3026 ● http://www.appliancerepair.net

Whirlpool®, Kitchenaid®, Roper®, Estate®, and Design 2000® are registered trademarks of Whirlpool Properties, Inc., Benton Harbor, Michigan, USA.

Kenmore® is a registered trademark of Sears, Roebuck and Co., Chicago, Illinois USA.

Special Thanks to technical consultants Dick Miller, Jose Hernandez, and Woody Randolph, whose collective decades of experience as field appliance service technicians are reflected in the technical information and procedures described in this publication.

Distributed exclusively by:
EB Marketing Group
597 N. Lake Havasu Ave.
Lake Havasu City, AZ 86403
Phone: (800) 400-3026 Fax (800) 400-4419

Printed in the United States of America

HOW TO USE THIS BOOK

STEP 1: READ THE DISCLAIMERS ON THE PREVIOUS PAGE. This book is intended for use by people who have a bit of mechanical experience or aptitude, and just need a little coaching when it comes to appliances. If you don't fit that category, don't use this book! We're all bloomin' lawyers these days, y'know? If you break something or hurt yourself, no one is responsible but **YOU**; not the author, the publisher, the guy or the store who sold you this book, or anyone else. Only **YOU** are responsible, and just by using this book, you're agreeing to that. If you don't understand the disclaimers, get a lawyer to translate them **before** you start working.

Read the safety and repair precautions in section 1-5. These should help you avoid making too many *really* bad mistakes.

STEP 2: READ CHAPTERS 1 & 2: Everything else in this book flows from chapters 1 and 2. If you don't read them, you won't be able to properly diagnose your washer.

Know what kind of washer you have and basically how it works. When you go to the appliance parts dealer, have the nameplate information at hand. Have the proper tools at hand, and know how to use them.

STEP 3: READ CHAPTER 3 OR 4 ABOUT YOUR SPECIFIC MODEL.

STEP 4: FIX THE BLOOMIN' THING! If you can, of course. If you're just too confused, or if the book recommends calling a technician for a complex operation, call one.

WHAT THIS BOOK WILL DO FOR YOU
(and what it won't!)

This book **will** tell you how to fix the most common problems with the most common brands of domestic (household) top-loading washing machines. (This represents 95+ percent of all repairs that the average handyman or service tech will run into.)

This book **will not** tell you how to fix your industrial or commercial or any very large washing machine. The support and control systems for such units are usually very similar in function to those of smaller units, but vastly different in design, service and repair.

We **will** show you the easiest and/or fastest method of diagnosing and repairing your washer.

We **will not necessarily** show you the cheapest way of doing something. Sometimes, when the cost of a part is just a few dollars, we advocate replacing the part rather than re-building it. We also sometimes advocate replacement of an inexpensive part, whether it's good or bad, as a simplified method of diagnosis or as a preventive measure.

We **will** use only the simplest of tools; tools that a well-equipped home mechanic is likely to have and to know how to use, including a VOM.

We **will not** advocate your buying several hundred dollars' worth of exotic equipment or special tools, or getting advanced technical training to make a one-time repair. It will usually cost you less to have a professional perform this type of repair. Such repairs represent only a very small percentage of all needed repairs.

We **do not** discuss electrical or mechanical theories. There are already many very well-written textbooks on these subjects and most of them are not likely to be pertinent to the job at hand; fixing your washer!

We **do** discuss rudimentary mechanical systems and simple electrical circuits.

We expect you to be able to look at a part and remove it if the mounting bolts and/or connections are obvious. If the mounting mechanism is complicated or hidden, or there are tricks to removing or installing something, we'll tell you about it.

You are expected to know what certain electrical and mechanical devices are, what they do in general, and how they work. For example, switches, relays, motors, solenoids, cams, clutches, brakes, pullies, idlers, belts, helical shafts, radial and thrust (axial) bearings, flex-ible motor couplings, splines, water valves, water and oil seals, centrifugal pumps, and pressure diaphragms. If you do not know what these things do, learn them BEFORE you start working on your washer.

You should know how to cut, strip, and splice wire with crimp-on connectors, wire nuts and electrical tape. You should know how to measure voltage and how to test for continuity with a VOM (Volt-Ohm Meter). If you have an ammeter, you should know how and where to measure the current in amps. If you don't know how to use these meters, there's a brief course on how to use them (for *our* purposes *only*) in Chapter 1. See section 1-4 before you buy either or both of these meters.

A given procedure was only included in this book if it passed the following criteria:

　1) The job is something that the average couch potato can complete in one afternoon, with no prior knowledge of the machine, with tools a normal home handyman is likely to have.

　2) The parts and/or special tools required to complete the job are easily found and not too expensive.

　3) The problem is a common one; occuring more frequently than just one out of a hundred machines.

Costly repairs which are included in this book if they pass the following criteria:

　1)The cost of the repair is still far less than replacing the machine or calling a professional service technician, and

　2) The repair is likely to yield a machine that will operate satisfactorily for several more years, or at least long enough to justify the cost.

　In certain parts of the book, the author expresses an opinion as to whether the current value of a particular machine warrants making the repair or "scrapping" the machine. Such opinions are to be construed as opinions ONLY and they are NOT to be construed as legal advice. The decision as to whether to take a particular machine out of service depends on a number of factors that the author cannot possibly know and has no control over; therefore, the responsibility for such a decision rests solely with the person making the decision.

　I'm sure that a physicist reading this book could have a lot of fun tearing it apart because of my deliberate avoidance and misuse of technical terms. However, this manual is written to simplify the material and inform the novice, not to appease the scientist.

　*NOTE:The diagnosis and repair procedures in this manual do not necessarily apply to brand-new units, newly-installed units or recently relocated units. Although they **may** posess the problems described in this manual, washers that have recently been installed or moved are subject to special considerations not taken into account in this manual for the sake of simplicity. Such special considerations include installation parameters, installation location, the possibility of manufacturing or construction defects, damage in transit, and others.*

　This manual was designed to assist the novice technician in the repair of home (domestic) washers that have been operating successfully for an extended period of months or years and have only recently stopped operating properly, with no major change in installation parameters or location.

Table of Contents

CHAPTER 3
WHIRLPOOL / KENMORE BELT DRIVE

CHAPTER 4
WHIRLPOOL / KENMORE DIRECT DRIVE

Chapter 1

WASHER IDENTIFICATION
TOOLS AND SAFETY
TIPS AND TRICKS

1-1 WASHER IDENTIFICATION

Appliance companies, like most other major industries, have their share of takeovers, buyouts and cross-brand agreements.

Some manufacturers "private label" their machines for large department stores. Sears' Kenmore is such an example. Sears does not manufacture appliances. Kenmore washers are, and always have been, private-labelled "Whirlpool" washers, both belt-drive and direct-drive.

BELT DRIVE MACHINES:

From the 50's into the early 80's, Whirlpool used essentially the same old, dependable, bullet-proof design. They are known in the parts houses as "Whirlpool belt-drive" models.

DIRECT DRIVE MACHINES:

In the early 80's, Whirlpool began manufacturing their "Design 2000" washers. These are known in the parts houses as "Whirlpool direct drive" models.

In the '90's, Whirlpool purchased KitchenAid. KitchenAid and Roper machines are direct-drive.

1-2 BEFORE YOU START

Find yourself a good appliance parts dealer. You can find them in the Yellow Pages under the following headings:

- APPLIANCES, HOUSEHOLD, MAJOR
- APPLIANCES, PARTS AND SUPPLIES
- REFRIGERATORS, DOMESTIC
- APPLIANCES, HOUSEHOLD, REPAIR AND SERVICE

Call a few of them and ask if they are a repair service, or if they sell parts, or both. Ask them if they offer free advice with the parts they sell. (Occasionally, stores that offer parts *and* service will not want to give you advice.) Often, the parts counter men are ex-technicians who got tired of the pressure of going into peoples' houses and selling a job. They can be your best friends; however, you don't want to badger them with TOO many questions, so know your basics before you start asking questions.

Some parts houses may offer service too. Be careful! They may try to talk you out of even *trying* to fix your own washer. They'll tell you it's too complicated, then in the same breath, "guide" you to their service department. Who are you gonna believe, me or them? Not all service/parts places are this way, however. If they genuinely *try* to help you fix it yourself and you find that you can't fix the problem, they may be a really good place to look for service.

When you go into the store, have ready your make, model and serial number from the *nameplate* of the washer.

NAMEPLATE INFORMATION

The metal nameplate information is usually found in one of the places shown in Figure 1-1:

A) Along the bottom panel; on the left or right corner.

B) Inside or underneath the lid.

C) Somewhere on the back of the washer.

D) Side or top of the console

If all else fails, check the original papers that came with your washer when it was new. They should contain the model number SOMEWHERE.

If you have absolutely NO information about the washer anywhere, make sure you bring your old part to the parts store with you. Sometimes they can match an old part by looks or by part number.

1-3 TOOLS (Figure 1-2)

The tools that you may need (depending on the diagnosis) are listed below. Some are optional. The reason for the option is explained.

For certain repairs, you will need a special tool. These are inexpensively available from your appliance parts dealer. They are listed in this book as needed.

SCREWDRIVERS: Both flat and phillips head; two or three different sizes of each. It is best to have at least a stubby, 4" and 6" sizes.

NUTDRIVERS: You will need at least a 1/4" and a 5/16" nut driver. 4" or 6" ones should suffice, but it's better to have stubbies, too.

ELECTRICAL PLIERS or STRIPPERS and DIAGONAL CUTTING PLIERS: For cutting and stripping small electrical wire.

VOM(VOLT-OHM METER): For testing circuits. If you do not have one, get one. An inexpensive one will suffice, as long as it has both "A.C. Voltage" and "Resistance" (i.e. R x 1, R x 10, etc.) settings on the dial. It will do for our purposes. If you are inexperienced in using one, get an analog (pointer) type (as opposed to a digital.)

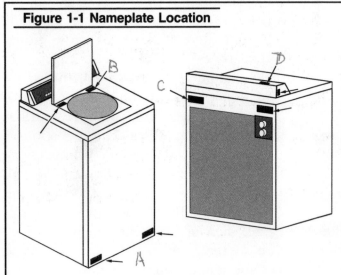

Figure 1-1 Nameplate Location

ALLIGATOR JUMPERS (sometimes called a "CHEATER" or "CHEATER WIRE"): small gauge (14-16 gauge or so) and about 12 to 18 inches long; for testing electrical circuits. Available at your local electronics store. Cost: a few bucks for 4 or 5 of them.

SYRINGE TYPE TURKEY BASTER: For cleaning fill hose and fill solenoid valve strainer screens.

SOCKET WRENCHES

FLASHLIGHT

OPEN END/BOX WRENCHES

BUTT CONNECTORS, CRIMPERS, WIRE NUTS AND ELECTRICAL TAPE: For splicing small wire.

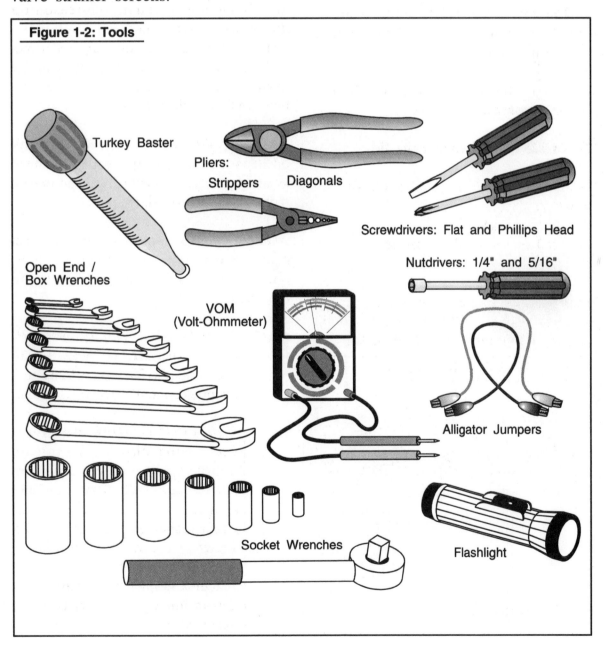

Figure 1-2: Tools

Turkey Baster

Pliers:

Strippers   Diagonals

Screwdrivers: Flat and Phillips Head

Nutdrivers: 1/4" and 5/16"

Open End / Box Wrenches

VOM (Volt-Ohmmeter)

Alligator Jumpers

Socket Wrenches

Flashlight

OPTIONAL TOOLS (Figure 1-3)

SNAP-AROUND AMMETER: For determining if electrical components are energized. Quite useful; but a bit expensive, and there are alternate methods. If you have one, use it; otherwise, don't bother getting one.

CORDLESS POWER SCREWDRIVER OR DRILL/DRIVER WITH MAGNETIC SCREWDRIVER AND NUTDRIVER TIPS: For pulling off panels held in place by many screws. It can save you lots of time and hassle.

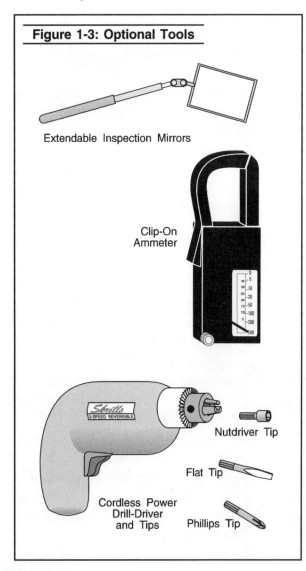

Figure 1-3: Optional Tools

Extendable Inspection Mirrors

Clip-On Ammeter

Nutdriver Tip

Flat Tip

Cordless Power Drill-Driver and Tips

Phillips Tip

EXTENDABLE INSPECTION MIRROR: For seeing difficult places beneath the washer and behind panels.

1-4 BASIC REPAIR AND SAFETY PRECAUTIONS

1) Always de-energize (pull the plug or trip the breaker on) any washer that you're disassembling. If you need to re-energize the washer to perform a test, make sure any bare wires or terminals are taped or insulated. Energize the unit only long enough to perform whatever test you're performing, then disconnect the power again.

2) To work underneath the washer sometimes requires leaning the washer back against the wall at a 30- to 45-degree angle. When you do, always block up one corner of the washer as shown in Figure 1-7. NEVER DO THIS ALONE! Always have someone standing by to help you while you work beneath the washer, in case it comes down on you.

3) If the manual advocates replacing the part, REPLACE IT!! You might find, say, a solenoid that has jammed for no apparent reason. Sometimes you can clean it out and lubricate it, and get it going again. The key words here are *apparent reason*. There is a reason that it stopped--you can bet on it--and if you get it going and re-install it, you are running a very high risk that it will stop again. If *that* happens, you will have to start repairing your washer *all* over again. It may only act up when it is hot, or it may be bent slightly...there are a hundred different "what if's." Very few of the parts mentioned in this book will cost you over ten or twenty dollars. Replace the part.

4) If you must lay the washer over on its side, front or back, first make sure that you are not going to break anything off, such as a drain hose or fill valve. Lay an old blanket on the floor to protect the floor and the finish of the washer. And for goodness' sake, make sure you drain the thing completely first!

5) Always replace the green (ground) leads when you remove an electrical component. They're there for a reason. And NEVER EVER remove the third (ground) prong in the main power plug!

6) When opening the washer cabinet or console, remember that the sheet metal parts are have very sharp edges. Wear gloves, and be careful not to cut your hands!

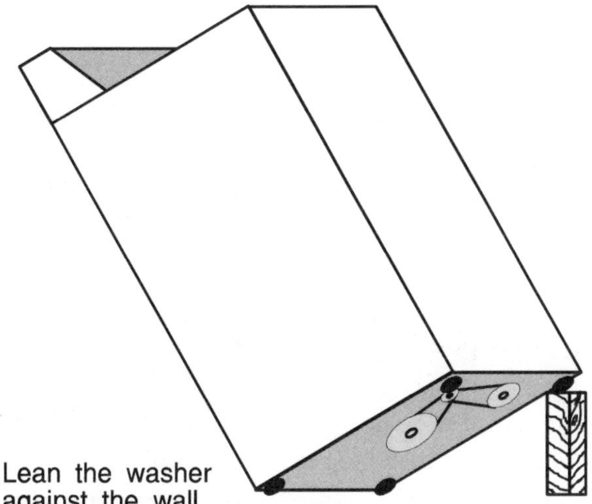

1-5 TIPS & TRICKS

Following are a few hard-earned pearls of wisdom:

1) When testing for your power supply from a wall outlet, plug in a small appliance such as a shaver or blow dryer. If you're not getting full power out of the outlet, you'll know it right away.

2) If you just can't get that agitator unstuck, your appliance parts dealer has a device called an Agi-Tamer for just such an occurrence. It's basically a heavy-duty rubber balloon that fits under the agitator, and uses water pressure to lift it upwards from underneath.

3) If you need to drain the tub (usually because your pump isn't pumping out) most folks try to bail it out. That's a wet, messy, yucky job, and not very thorough.

Try this instead: use your garden hose as a siphon.

However, when you do, another problem arises: did you ever try to suck a charge of wash water through a fifty-foot garden hose? If you can, you've got one heckuva set of lungs. And what happens when that nice, week-old dirty wash water reaches your mouth?

You guessed it: there's a better way.

What's the point in sucking the water through the hose? To get rid of the air in the hose, right? Well, instead of using *lung suction* to do that, let's use *house pressure*.

Figure 1-7: Leaning the Washer Against the Wall

To access belts or other parts underneath the washer:

Lean the washer against the wall at a 30 to 45 degree angle and block up the corner with a wood block

CAUTION: ALWAYS HAVE A HELPER STANDING BY IN CASE THE WASHER STARTS TO COME DOWN ON YOU!!!

Leave your garden hose connected to the faucet, and put the other end of it in the washer tub. Turn the faucet on for a few seconds, until it stops bubbling in the tub. The air is gone now, right?

Kink the garden hose so you don't lose the water charge, and disconnect it from the faucet. When you're sure the faucet end of the hose is lower than the

bottom of the washer tub, release the kink in the hose. The tub will drain, almost completely, in just a few minutes. No muss, no fuss.

1-6 HOW TO USE A VOM AND AMMETER

Many home handymen are very intimidated by electricity. It's true that diagnosing and repairing electrical circuits requires a *bit* more care than most operations, due to the danger of getting shocked. But there is no mystery or voodoo about the things we'll be doing. Remember the rule in section 1-4 (1); while you are working on a circuit, energize the circuit only long enough to perform whatever test you're performing, then take the power back off it to perform the repair. You need not be concerned with any theory, like what an ohm is, or what a volt is. You will only need to be able to set the VOM onto the right scale, touch the test leads to the right place and read the meter.

In using the VOM (Volt-Ohm Meter) for our purposes, the two test leads are always plugged into the "+" and "-" holes on the VOM. (Some VOMs have more than two holes.)

1-6(a) TESTING VOLTAGE (Figure 1-4)

Set the dial of the VOM on the lowest VAC scale (A.C. Voltage) over 120 volts. For example, if there's a 50 setting and a 250 setting on the VAC dial, use the 250 scale, because 250 is the lowest setting over 120 volts.

Touch the two test leads to the two

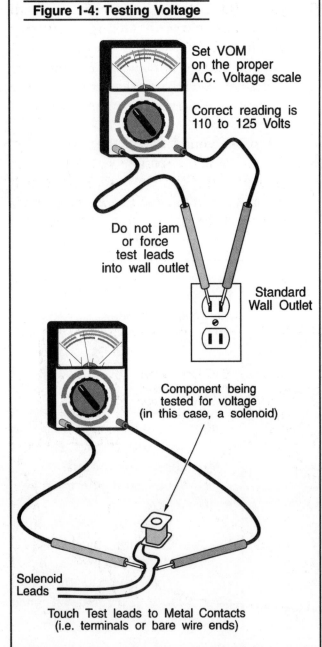

Figure 1-4: Testing Voltage

Set VOM on the proper A.C. Voltage scale

Correct reading is 110 to 125 Volts

Do not jam or force test leads into wall outlet

Standard Wall Outlet

Component being tested for voltage (in this case, a solenoid)

Solenoid Leads

Touch Test leads to Metal Contacts (i.e. terminals or bare wire ends)

metal contacts of a live power source, like a wall outlet or the terminals of the motor that you're testing for voltage. (*Do not* **jam** *the test leads into a wall outlet!*) If you are getting power through the VOM, the meter will jump up and steady on a reading. You *may* have to convert the scale in your head. For example, if you're using the 250 volt dial setting and the meter has a "25" scale, simply divide by 10; 120 volts would be "12" on the meter.

1-6(b) TESTING FOR CONTINUITY (Figure 1-5)

Don't let the word "continuity" scare you. It's derived from the word "continuous." In an electrical circuit, electricity has to flow *from* a power source back *to* that power source. If there is any break in the circuit, it is not continuous, and it has no continuity.

"Good" continuity means that there is no break in the circuit.

For example, if you were testing a solenoid to see if it was burned out, you would try putting a small amount of power through the solenoid. If it was burned out, there would be a break in the circuit, the electricity wouldn't flow, and your meter would show no continuity.

That is what the resistance part of your VOM does; it provides a small electrical current (using batteries within the VOM) and measures how fast the current is flowing. For our purposes, it doesn't matter how *fast* the current is flowing; only that there *is* current flow.

To use your VOM to test continuity, set the dial on (resistance) R x 1, or whatever the lowest setting is. Touch the metal parts of the test leads together and read the meter. It should peg the meter all the way on the right side of the

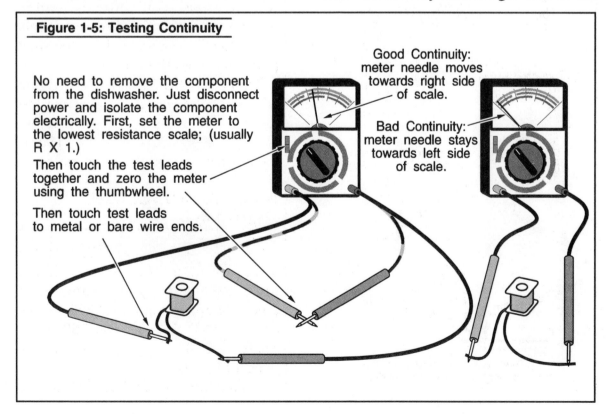

Figure 1-5: Testing Continuity

No need to remove the component from the dishwasher. Just disconnect power and isolate the component electrically. First, set the meter to the lowest resistance scale; (usually R X 1.)

Then touch the test leads together and zero the meter using the thumbwheel.

Then touch test leads to metal or bare wire ends.

Good Continuity: meter needle moves towards right side of scale.

Bad Continuity: meter needle stays towards left side of scale.

scale, towards "0" on the meter's "resistance" scale. If the meter does not read zero resistance, adjust the thumbwheel on the front of the VOM until it *does* read zero. If you cannot get the meter to read zero, the battery in the VOM is low; replace it.

If you are testing, say, a solenoid, first make sure that the solenoid leads are not connected to anything, especially a power source. If the solenoid's leads are still connected to something, you may get a reading through that something. If there is still live power on the item you're testing for continuity, you will burn out your VOM instantly and possibly shock yourself.

Touch the two test leads to the two bare wire ends or terminals of the solenoid. You can touch the ends of the wires and test leads with your hands if necessary to get better contact. The voltage that the VOM batteries put out is very low, and you will not be shocked. If there is NO continuity, the meter won't move. If there is GOOD continuity, the meter will move toward the right side of the scale and steady on a reading. This is the resistance reading and it doesn't concern us; we only care that we show good continuity. If the meter moves only very little and stays towards the left side of the scale, that's BAD continuity; the solenoid is no good.

If you are testing a switch, you will show little or no resistance (good continuity) when the switch is closed, and NO continuity when the switch is open. If you do not, the switch is bad.

1-6(c) AMMETERS

Ammeters are a little bit more complex to explain without going into a lot of electrical theory. If you own an ammeter, you probably already know how to use it.

If you don't, don't get one. Ammeters are expensive. And for *our* purposes, there are other ways to determine what an ammeter tests for. If you don't own one, skip this section.

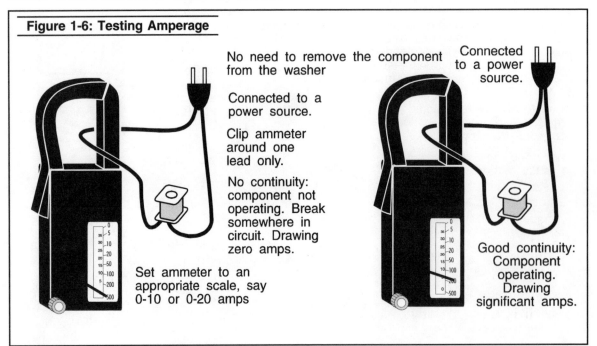

Figure 1-6: Testing Amperage

No need to remove the component from the washer

Connected to a power source.

Clip ammeter around one lead only.

No continuity: component not operating. Break somewhere in circuit. Drawing zero amps.

Set ammeter to an appropriate scale, say 0-10 or 0-20 amps

Connected to a power source.

Good continuity: Component operating. Drawing significant amps.

For our purposes, ammeters are simply a way of testing for continuity without having to cut into the system or to disconnect power from whatever it is we're testing.

Ammeters measure the current in amps flowing through a wire. The greater the current that's flowing *through* a wire, the greater the density of the magnetic field it produces *around* the wire. The ammeter simply measures the strength of this magnetic field, and thus the amount of current, flowing through the wire. To determine continuity, for our purposes, we can simply isolate the component that we're testing (so we do not accidentally measure the current going through any other components) and see if there's *any* current flow.

To use your ammeter, first make sure that it's on an appropriate scale (0 to 10 or 20 amps will do). Isolate a wire leading directly to the component you're testing. Put the ammeter loop around that wire and read the meter. (Figure 1-6)

Chapter 2

PROBLEMS COMMON TO BOTH DESIGNS

Washing machine designs vary widely, but there are *some* things that *all* washers have in common. For example, all washers have an electric motor. All washers have both spin and agitate cycles. And since both cycles are driven by the same electric motor, all washers have some sort of mechanism to change between the two.

All washers must also have a way of filling the tub with wash water and a way of draining out used wash water. And incidental to this, all washers must have a way of controlling water level in the tub, to prevent spillage by overfill or by centrifugal force during the spin cycle.

All washers must (by law) have a mechanism that brakes the spinning basket at the end of the spin cycle, or else a lid lock to prevent the lid from being opened during or shortly after the spin cycle.

And last but not least, all washers must have a timer that controls and coordinates the start, stop and duration of the various cycles.

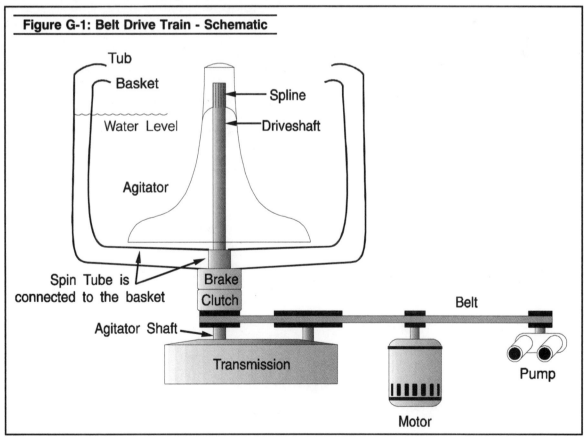

Figure G-1: Belt Drive Train - Schematic

Tub

Basket

Spline

Water Level

Driveshaft

Agitator

Spin Tube is connected to the basket

Brake

Clutch

Belt

Agitator Shaft

Transmission

Pump

Motor

2-1 CYCLES

FILL CYCLE

During the FILL cycle, a solenoid-operated water mixing valve opens and allows hot or cold water (or both) to enter the tub. There is no pump operating at this time; the tub fills strictly from house pressure. Similarly, there is no heater in your washer; the heat comes from the water heater in your home.

When the water in the tub reaches a certain level, a pressure switch closes the water solenoid valve(s).

WASH/RINSE (AGITATION) CYCLE

After the water valve closes, an electric motor starts which drives the transmission, sometimes through a belt, and in some cases through a clutch arrangement, too. The transmission converts the rotary motion of the motor to the back-and-forth motion of the agitator. A driveshaft extends from the top of the transmission to the agitator, where it is connected to the agitator, usually by a spline. (See Figure G-1.)

Agitation will continue for a certain amount of time, which is controlled by the timer. During agitation, some washers use their pump to circulate water, sucking it from the bottom of the tub and pumping it to the top of the tub. The pump is driven by the same electric motor.

Also during the agitation cycle, bleach or softener may be automatically added. This is usually done by a solenoid valve that allows some of the recirculated water to flush out the bleach or softener dispenser. In some models there is no water circulation involved; the solenoid simply opens a valve or door that lets the dispenser contents drop into the wash water. The timer tells this solenoid valve when to open.

SPIN AND DRAIN CYCLES

After agitation comes a drain cycle, sometimes combined with a spin cycle. During the drain cycle, the pump sucks water from the tub and sends it down the drain. During the spin cycle, the same motor that drove the agitator now drives a spin tube which is concentric with the agitator shaft. (See Figure G-1) The spin tube spins the basket, slinging excess water out of the clothes by centrifugal force. There is a clutch arrangement which allows the basket to come up to speed slowly. This prevents a heavy load from being thrown onto the motor suddenly. It also allows a "pre-pump" action; the water has a

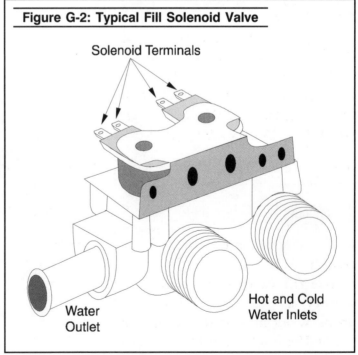

Figure G-2: Typical Fill Solenoid Valve

Solenoid Terminals

Water Outlet

Hot and Cold Water Inlets

chance to drain out of the tub before the basket gets up to speed, preventing the water from overflowing the edge of the tub by centrifugal force.

Some brands have a partial drain cycle only, then refill and agitate again. Some start spinning and draining at the same time. Some only drain until the water reaches a certain level, then start spinning. Most brands have lid switches that prevent the basket from spinning when the lid is open. Some brands have a lid lock that prevents you from opening the lid when the basket is spinning.

At the end of the spin cycle, or whenever the lid is lifted, most models have a braking arrangement that stops the tub from spinning. This helps to prevent people from accidently sticking their hands into a spinning basket.

CAUTION: NEVER BYPASS THE LID SWITCH, EXCEPT FOR TEST PURPOSES. IF IT IS DEFECTIVE, INSTALL A NEW ONE. THEY ARE THERE FOR A REASON. NO JOKE: I PERSONALLY HAVE A NEPHEW WHOSE ARM WAS TORN OFF (AT 2 YEARS OLD) BECAUSE OF A BYPASSED LID SWITCH!

2-2 FILL SYSTEM

The basic components of the fill system are the hoses, the fill valve, and the pressure or float switch.

The fill valve (Figure G-2) is simply a solenoid valve that opens when activated and allows hot and/or cold water to flow into the tub. Most modern washers use dual solenoid valves, which have both hot and cold solenoids in one valve body. When *warm* water is desired, both valves open to mix hot and cold.

In the newest digital washers, water temperature may be controlled by a "thermistor." A thermistor is a variable resistor; a resistor whose resistance varies according to what temperature it senses. The thermistor's signal goes to the washer's control board (computer,) which opens or closes hot and cold water valves to control the incoming water temperature.

When the water in the tub reaches the desired level, the pressure or float switch closes the circuit to the fill

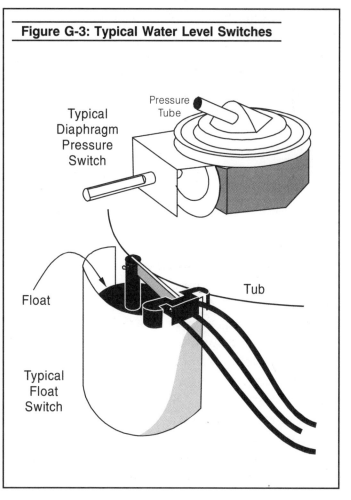

Figure G-3: Typical Water Level Switches

(handwritten margin note:) SEE NOTE 3.5 - LID SWITCH BROKE, FELL ONTO TUB. NO DRAIN CYCLE, NO PUMP, NO SPIN.

valve. Float switches are pretty rare; you'll find them only in older washers. A diaphragm-type pressure switch is more common. Typical float and pressure switches are shown in Figure G-3. A few old washers used a pressure switch mounted on the BOTTOM of the tub; these are known as water weight switches. They are rare.

DIAGNOSIS

If your washer is not filling properly, or is overflowing, there could be several reasons.

SLOW OR NO FILL, OR WATER TOO HOT OR TOO COLD

If your washer is filling very slowly or not at all, or the water temperature is always too hot or too cold, check the fill hose and valve strainers. These are little screens placed in the fill hose and/

Figure G-4: Fill Strainer Screens

Flush Strainer Screen with Turkey Baster

Use Pan To Catch Runoff

Screen Sometimes in Hose End

Strainer Screens

or water valve to prevent rust and scale from your house's piping system from getting into the water valve. The strainers can get clogged up over time and prevent water flow.

Shut off the water valves and remove

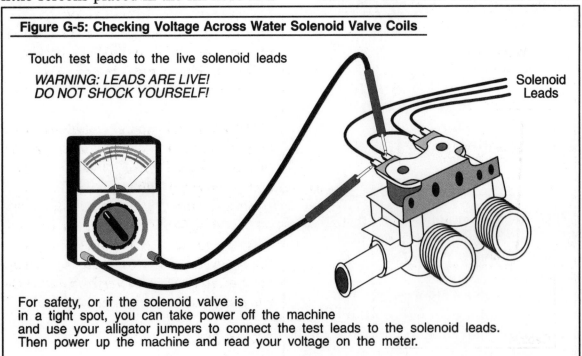

Figure G-5: Checking Voltage Across Water Solenoid Valve Coils

Touch test leads to the live solenoid leads

WARNING: LEADS ARE LIVE! DO NOT SHOCK YOURSELF!

Solenoid Leads

For safety, or if the solenoid valve is in a tight spot, you can take power off the machine and use your alligator jumpers to connect the test leads to the solenoid leads. Then power up the machine and read your voltage on the meter.

the hoses. Look into the both ends of each hose and into the water valve mounted on the washer. In at least one of the three places you should see a strainer screen. (Figure G-4) If it is clogged, you can try cleaning it out with a toothbrush and/or a turkey baster. If you cannot clean the screen sufficiently, you may need to replace it. In some instances, the screen is non-removable, and you will need to replace the hose or valve. Neither is very expensive.

When re-installing the hoses, always use new hose washers. Also, take care not to overtighten the hose on the plastic threads of the solenoid valve; tighten just enough to stop it from leaking. If there is any question about the watertight integrity of the hose, replace it. A hose costs a lot less than a new floor or carpeting, which is what you'll be buying if it breaks while you're not home.

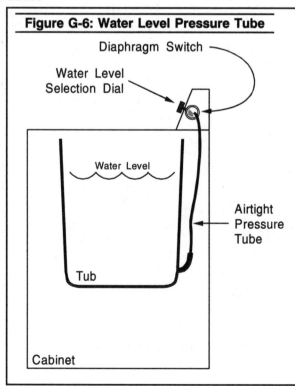

Figure G-6: Water Level Pressure Tube

Diaphragm Switch

Water Level Selection Dial

Water Level

Airtight Pressure Tube

Tub

Cabinet

If the strainers look O.K., set your temperature control to "warm" and set your timer in the fill cycle. Raise the lid of the washer and depress any lid switch with a pen or screwdriver. Feel the water entering the washer. If it is too hot or too cold, or if no water is coming out at all, test for voltage across each solenoid coil of the water valve as shown in figure G-5. It should read 110 to 125 volts.

If so, you're getting power to your valve, but it's not opening. Replace the valve.

If you're not getting power to the valve, refer to the wiring diagram for your machine (see section 2-6) and trace the source of the interruption. Sometimes it's a broken wire, but more commonly, there will be a problem with the water level switch, timer, lid switch, or temperature switch. Replace the defective switch.

If your washer is a late-model digital machine with a fill thermistor, a defective thermistor might be sending the wrong signal to the control board. Replacing the thermistor (they're not too expensive) will usually solve the problem. The control board may also be defective.

CAUTION: On some machines, you must raise the top of the cabinet to get to the solenoid valve. If your washer has a mercury-tube type lid switch, raising the top of the cabinet may have the same effect on the lid switch as raising the lid. Your washer may not fill or cycle. You will need to jumper the mercury switch to perform any tests when the cabinet top is raised.

OVERFILL

As the tub fills, water pressure increases at the bottom of the tub. This pressure is transmitted to the diaphragm in the water level switch by a rubber or plastic tube. (Figure G-6) When the tub reaches the right level, the diaphragm trips the switch, closing the solenoid fill valve and starting the agitate cycle.

If the tube or diaphragm is leaking badly, the water level switch will not sense any pressure, and thus will not shut off the water flow, so the tub will overflow. If this tube is leaking *slowly*, the washer may exhibit odd fill symptoms. For example, depending on how fast the air leak is, the washer may fill and start agitating, then stop agitating and fill some more, then agitate some more, and so forth, until the washer overfills.

CAUTION: Whenever you remove the tube from the switch, or insert the tube onto the switch, there cannot be any water in the tub or tube. Before you insert the tube onto the switch, blow into the tube first, to clear it of any water that might have gotten in it. ANY WATER REMAINING IN THE TUBE WILL CAUSE YOUR WASHER TO OVERFILL, OR PROBABLY EVEN TO OVERFLOW!

Also test the water level switch electrically, as described in section 2-6(b).

DOES NOT STOP FILLING, AND/OR WATER LEVEL KEEPS GOING DOWN

If the house washer drain starts backing up, you get a rooter and clear the drain, right? But *some* people would just seal it up so it couldn't overflow, instead of clearing the drain, as they should. (Now, *WE* wouldn't do that, would we, folks?)

But that air break between the washer's drain hose and the house's drain pipe is important. If there is no air break, and the drain system fills with water, it can actually start siphoning water right through the pump and down the drain. Depending on how bad the drain is backing up, the washer might never fill completely; the solenoid valve will just stay open and water will just keep siphoning straight out the drain. Or, if the drain is a little more clogged and the water is flowing more slowly, the washer might fill and start agitating, but stop agitating after a few minutes and fill some more. This fill-agitate-fill-agitate cycle will continue for as long as the agitate cycle lasts. And since the power to the timer motor is being interrupted, the wash and rinse cycles may seem unusually long.

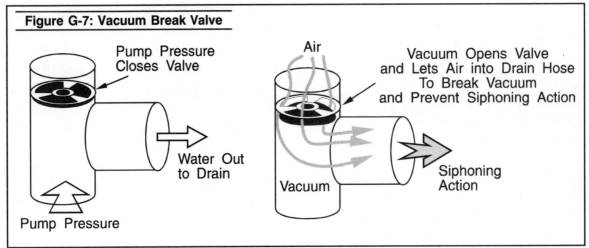

Figure G-7: Vacuum Break Valve

Pump Pressure Closes Valve

Water Out to Drain

Pump Pressure

Air

Vacuum Opens Valve and Lets Air into Drain Hose To Break Vacuum and Prevent Siphoning Action

Vacuum

Siphoning Action

There is a solution, even if you don't want to root out the drain blockage as you should. Your appliance parts dealer has a drain line vacuum break valve, available for just a few bucks. (Figure G-7) You can cut into your drain line and install one of these vacuum breaks pretty easily.

When the drain line is under pressure, (like when the pump is pumping out) the flapper valve closes and no leakage occurs. When the drain line is under a vacuum (like when the drain is trying to siphon it) the flapper valve opens and air is allowed into the drain line, breaking the siphoning action.

2-3 PUMP; DRAIN AND RECIRCULATION SYSTEMS

The pump can perform several functions. In all washers, it is used to pump water out of the tub at the end of an agitate or soak cycle. In some washers, it also circulates water during the agitate cycle. It may also provide flush water for a bleach or softener dispenser. Therefore, the pump *may* be required to pump in two different directions or more during a cycle.

Some brands and/or models accomplish this by using two different pump impellers in one body; the pump body will have two inlets and two outlets. Others use a solenoid-activated butterfly valve in the pump body to re-direct the waterflow. Still others use a direct-reversing pump; the motor driving the pump turns in the opposite direction, and the pump pumps in the opposite direction.

DIAGNOSIS

Sometimes the most obvious answers are the first ones overlooked. If the tub isn't draining, first check the drain system. Check the drain hose to make sure it isn't kinked. Also check any lint filter that may be installed. On some Whirlpool/Kenmore models, there is also a side-check valve at the tub outlet that can get clogged.

There aren't too many things that can go wrong with a pump. The pump bearings can seize, stopping it from turning. The pump can be jammed by socks or other small items. The impeller blades can break off due to junk entering the pump; if this happens, the pump may seize up, or it may just stop pumping. The usual solution is to replace the pump.

But the *symptoms* of a pump failure are something else altogether. If the pump locks up, and the motor is still trying to turn it, *something's* gotta give. If the pump is belt-driven, the pulley driving the pump may shear off, or the belt may break. The belt may ride over the locked pulley, or the motor pulley will continue turning under the belt; this will burn the belt and possibly break it. There may even be enough tension on the belt to stop the motor from turning.

The symptoms can be confusing. For example, a common complaint about a Whirlpool belt-drive washer is that it isn't spinning, accompanied by a strong burning smell. The problem is almost always a pump that's locked up. The washer doesn't enter the spin cycle because the spin is interlocked with the drain cycle. This means that the basket won't start spinning until the water is partially drained. The burning smell comes from the rubber belt, which is riding over the motor pulley or locked pump pulley.

NOTE: If you EVER find a broken belt, check for a locked pump, transmission or other pulley before replacing the belt.

If you suspect that something is jamming the pump, drain the tub and pull the hoses off the pump. Look into the hoses and the pump and pull out whatever is jamming it. If you can't see anything jamming the pump, feel around the inside of the pump inlets and outlets with a pair of needlenose pliers. If all else fails, and you still can't find the jam, pull the pump out of the machine and check it.

For specific information about pump replacement or service, see the chapter about *your* brand.

2-4 LEAKS

Although there are a few leaks common to all brands, most brands have leaks that are peculiar to their design. GE, Whirlpool, Maytag, and others all have common and well-known leak areas. After reading this section, see the chapter about specific brands for details.

A common "leak" zone is not a leak at all; the wall drain backs up and overflows onto the floor. This is commonly misdiagnosed as a leak. It can be difficult to diagnose; the problem may be intermittent. Depending on how badly the drain is clogged, there may be a little water or a lot, or it may only overflow every second or third load. While diagnosing a leak, do not be too quick to write this diagnosis off.

If you suspect that your drain is backing up, but you can't quite ever be there at the right time to *observe* the overflow, try this: wrap some toilet paper around the drain hose just above the wall drain pipe. If it backs up, the paper will get wet. Even if you're not there when it happens and the paper dries out, it will have crinkled up, and you'll know your drain's backing up.

If it isn't the drain, run the machine with a full load. Without moving the machine, get right down on the floor and look under the machine with a flashlight. Try to find the general area where water is dripping to the floor; front or back of the machine, left or right side.

Open the cabinet and look for mineral or soap deposits where there shouldn't be any. Trace the deposits in the natural direction of waterflow (against gravity or centrifugal force) back to the source of the leak. Fill the machine again and run it through a cycle or two. Be patient; use your eyes and your brains. There is no magic, easy way to detect a leak.

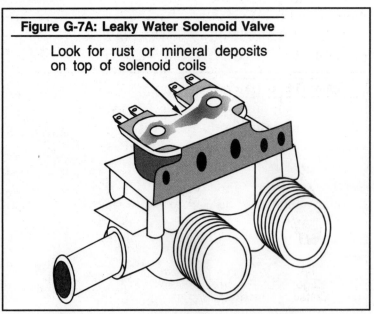

Figure G-7A: Leaky Water Solenoid Valve

Look for rust or mineral deposits on top of solenoid coils

The *usual* places are:

WATER VALVE: The guts of the fill solenoid valve sometimes will corrode. You may see water leaking from, or rust on the top of the solenoid. (See figure G-7A) Since the valves only open during a fill cycle, this may appear as an intermittent leak. The solution is to replace the valve.

PUMP: Usually from around the pulley seal. Some washer pumps have a hole that allows water to weep out when the seal starts to go bad. The solution is to replace or rebuild the pump.

BLEACH DISPENSERS: Bleach is *VERY* hard on plastic parts. If the bleach dispenser gets old and brittle, it can crack or break off, and the flush water can leak out. But since the dispenser may only be flushed at certain times in the cycle, this will appear as an intermittent leak. The solution is to replace the dispenser, or if you don't use it any more, plug the hose and seal the cracked dispenser with RTV (silicone seal.)

HOSES: Though hose leaks are a bit less common than other leaks, any hoses with a few too many miles on them may be suspect. Replace the hose.

TUB: If the tub is rotted through, it's probably time to replace the washer.

2-5 TRANSMISSION AND DRIVE TRAIN

Besides driving the pump in most washers, the main drive motor has two main functions: to spin the basket and reciprocate the agitator. One motor is used to do both.

Within the transmission there is typically a crank gear and connecting rod arrangement to provide the reciprocating motion to the agitator. However, some designs use a differential gear, slider, eccentric, or other design.

The spin motion comes directly from the rotary motion of the motor, through a clutch.

There must also be some mechanism to change between spin and agitate. There are two ways that this is most commonly done.

Whirlpool **belt drive** designs use solenoids to engage and disengage the clutch and transmission. The solenoid engages a clutch to turn the basket in the spin cycle. For the agitate cycle, this solenoid disengages the clutch and a different solenoid engages the transmission.

Whirlpool **direct-drive** machines use a direct-reversing motor. When the

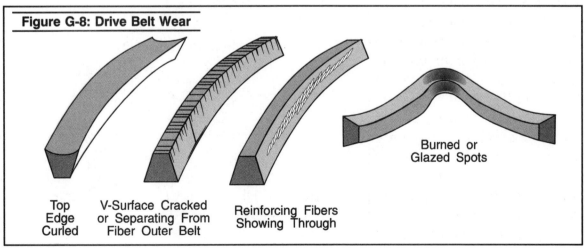

Figure G-8: Drive Belt Wear

Top Edge Curled

V-Surface Cracked or Separating From Fiber Outer Belt

Reinforcing Fibers Showing Through

Burned or Glazed Spots

motor turns one way, a mechanical arrangement within the transmission engages and spins the basket. When the motor reverses, the brake locks the basket and the transmission engages, so the agitator agitates.

Braking is "fail-safe;"" that is, if the solenoid fails (in a belt drive machine) or motor stops (in a direct drive machine) the brake will stop the basket automatically.

2-5(a) BELTS

Look closely at the surface of the belt. If you see any of the problems shown in figure G-8, replace it.

Broken or worn out belts are a common problem. See the chapter on *your* machine for specific details about changing the belt(s) on your model. If you **EVER** find a broken belt, check for a locked pump, transmission or other pulley before replacing the belt.

2-5(b) AGITATOR

If your washer is agitating weakly or not at all, the splines that connect it to the driveshaft may be stripped. It's a fairly common problem. Remove the agitator as described in the chapter specific to your washer. If the shaft *is* rotating but the agitator is *not*, replace the agitator or spline insert.

2-5(c) TRANSMISSIONS

Transmissions in general are pretty bullet-proof, and rarely experience problems beyond a little oil loss.

If your transmission is leaking oil badly, you basically have two options:

replace the transmission now, or keep running it until it runs out of oil and dies. Nobody I know of rebuilds transmissions themselves any more. It is far quicker and easier to just replace it with a rebuilt. See the chapter about your model for replacement details.

Occasionally, something will break inside the casing and lock the transmission, or prohibit its operation in one mode or another.

The symptoms may be similar to a locked pump; stalled motor, burning belt, etc.

To diagnose this, first unplug your washer. Try turning the motor by hand, or pull the belt so everything rotates. *Be careful you don't pinch your fingers between the belt and pulley!* Check to see that every pulley that the belt rides is rotating. It should be pretty stiff, but if you can't turn it at all, something is locked up. Disengage the drive system (remove the belt, etc.) Try to turn the transmission drive pulley with your hand. Also check the movement of the pump, and any tensioner or idler pulley that may be present.

Do not try to rebuild your own transmission. Typically, rebuilding requires special tools that drive the cost above that of buying a rebuilt transmission. Rebuilt trannies for the more popular models are inexpensively available from your parts dealer, and usually kept in stock.

2-6 TESTING ELECTRICAL COMPONENTS

Sometimes you need to read a wiring diagram, to make sure you are not forgetting to check something. Sometimes you just need to find out what color wire to look for to test a component. It is ESPECIALLY important in diagnosing a bad timer.

If you already know how to read a wiring diagram, you can skip this section. If you're one of those folks who's a bit timid around electricity, all I can say is read on, and don't be too nervous. It will come to you. You learned how to use a VOM in Chapter 1, right?

Look at figure G-9. The symbol used to represent each component is pretty universal, and each component should be labelled clearly on your diagram.

A few notes about reading a wiring diagram:

Notice that in some parts of the diagram, the lines are thicker than in other parts. The wiring and switches that are shown as thick lines are *inside* of the timer.

The small circles all over the diagram are terminals. These are places where you can disconnect the wire from the component for testing purposes.

If you see dotted or shaded lines around a group of wires, this is a switch assembly; for example, a water level, water temperature or motor speed switch assembly. It may also be the timer, but whatever it is, it should be clearly marked on the diagram. Any wiring enclosed by a shaded or dotted box is internal to a switch assembly and

must be tested as described in sections 2-6(c) and 2-6(d).

Switches may be numbered on the diagram, but that number will *not* be found on the switch. Those numbers are there to help you follow the timer sequencing chart. Don't worry about the timer sequencing chart. We are only concerned to see *if* the switch is opening and closing. We'll let the design engineers worry about exactly *when* it opens and closes.

To find (and test) a switch with a certain number, look for the color of the wires leading to the switch.

Wire colors are abbreviated; for example, BU means blue, BL or B

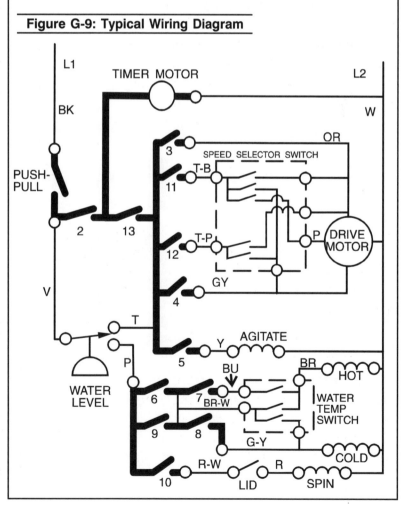

Figure G-9: Typical Wiring Diagram

means black, V means violet, T means tan. If you see a wire color with a dash or a slash, that means ―― with a ―― stripe. For example, OR-W means orange with a white stripe; G/P means green with a pink stripe.

NOTE: Green wires are ground wires and MUST be re-connected when removed.

Remember that for something to be energized, it must make a complete electrical circuit. You must be able to trace the path that the electricity will take, FROM the wall outlet back TO the wall outlet. This includes not only the component that you suspect, but all switches leading to it. In Figure G-9(a), L1 and L2 are the main power leads; they go directly to your wall plug.

Let's say you need to check out why the spin solenoid is not working. Following the gray-shaded circuit in figure G-9(a), the electricity flows through the black wire (L1) to the push-pull switch. This switch is located inside of the timer (you know this because it is drawn with thick lines) and it must be closed. The power then goes through the violet wire to the water level switch (which must have a LOW water level,) then through the pink wire back into the timer. Inside the timer, it goes through switch number 10. It then comes out of the timer in a red wire with a white stripe (R-W) that leads to the lid switch (which must be closed.) From the lid switch, it goes through a red wire to the spin solenoid. Finally it leaves the spin solenoid in a white wire, which leads back to the main power cord (L2).

If you're not sure whether a certain switch or component is a part of the circuit you're diagnosing, *assume* that it is and test it. For example, switches 3,4,11&12 all lead to the motor circuit. If you have a motor problem that you think you've traced to the timer, don't bother trying to figure out which switch goes to which part of the motor. Test all four; if any of the four switches is bad, you will need to replace the whole timer, anyway.

To test for the break in the circuit, simply isolate each part of the system (remove the wires from the terminals) and test for continuity. For example, to test the spin solenoid in our example, pull the red and white wires off the spin solenoid and test continuity across the solenoid terminals as described in section 2-6(a).

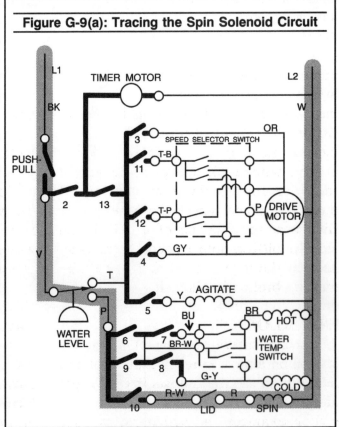

Figure G-9(a): Tracing the Spin Solenoid Circuit

The push-pull switch, and switch number 10 are shown in bold lines, so they are inside the timer. Looking at the diagram, the push-pull switch controls a lot of other things besides the spin solenoid. Since those things are working O.K., we know that the push-pull switch can't be the problem.

For now, let's ignore switch number 10. (Remember: the timer is the *last* thing you should check; see section 2-5(c).)

That leaves the water level switch, the lid switch, the spin solenoid itself, and the wiring.

Nine times out of ten, a component has gone bad. Test those first. Take power off the machine and check each switch and/or solenoid in the circuit as described in sections 2-5 (a) thru (e).

To check for a wire break, you would pull each end of a wire off the component and test for continuity through it. You may need to use jumpers to extend the wire; for example, if one end of the wire is in the control console and the other end in underneath the machine. If there is no continuity, there is a break in the wire! It will then be up to you to figure out exactly where that break is; there is no magic way. If you have a broken wire, look along the length of the wire for pinching or chafing. If there is a place where the wires move (like near the wigwag of a belt-driven Whirlpool/Kenmore,) check there first. Even if the insulation is O.K., the wire may be broken inside.

INTERLOCKS

Certain safety mechanisms are installed on almost every washer that can lead you to a misdiagnosis if you forget about them.

For example, a Whirlpool washer will pump out water if the lid is open, but it won't spin. So you've just replaced the pump, and you're standing there with the lid open, admiring how well it's pumping out, when you notice it still isn't spinning. You dive right back into the back of the washer, trying to figure out what you forgot to replace...and the only problem is that the lid is up. Don't laugh; I'd hate to admit to you how many times *I've* done it.

When diagnosing an electrical problem, there are many interlocks in the system that you need to check. (See section 2-7 below.) For example, if your basket won't spin at all, you will check all the obvious stuff (lid switch, spin clutch solenoid, transmission, etc.) But will you think to check the imbalance switch? If it fails, it will have the same effect as a failed lid switch. When tracing an electrical problem, check your wiring diagram to see if there may be any forgotten switches in the malfunctioning system.

Here are a few of the more common safety interlock mechanisms to watch out for:

LID SWITCH: Mentioned above, it prevents the basket from spinning while the washer lid is open. In some designs, it also prevents the tub from filling or the agitator from agitating while the lid is open. See the note about mercury lid switches in section 2-2.

IMBALANCE INTERLOCK: If the washer has detected a substantial imbalance in the load during the spin cycle, the motor will stop. Usually a buzzer will sound. To reset this interlock, the lid must be opened and closed or the timer turned off and back on.

(Presumably, you will redistribute the clothes, but it is not necessary to reset the interlock.)

WATER LEVEL INTERLOCK: On some washers, the basket will not start spinning until the water is nearly pumped out of the tub. The start of the spin cycle is dependent on the pump pumping out water and the water level switch sensing that the water level is low enough.

CAUTION: NEVER BYPASS A SAFETY INTERLOCK. THEY ARE THERE FOR A REASON.

2-6(a) SWITCHES AND SOLENOIDS

Testing switches and solenoids is pretty straightforward. Take all wires off the component and test resistance across it.

Switches should show good continuity when closed and no continuity when open.

Solenoids should show SOME resistance, but continuity should be good. If a solenoid shows no continuity, there's a break somewhere in the windings. If it shows no resistance, it's shorted.

2-6(b) WATER LEVEL SWITCHES

Water level diaphragm switches are usually shown on a wiring diagram by the symbol in figure G-10. The numbering or lettering of the terminals may differ, but basically all switches are tested the same way.

To test the switch, first fill the tub to the highest water level. Un-

plug the machine and set the water level switch on the lowest water level setting. Remove the three leads from the switch. Label the wires to make sure you get them back on the proper terminals.

In the example shown in figure G-10, a check for continuity should show the following:

TUB FULL: No continuity from V to P, continuity from V to T.

Re-attach the wires, plug in the machine and set the timer on "spin" or "drain." When the tub is pumped dry, stop the spin cycle and unplug the washer. Remove the wires from the water level switch and test continuity again. With an empty tub, the continuity should be reversed:

TUB EMPTY: Continuity from V to P, no continuity from V to T.

If you do not get these readings, the water level switch is bad, or there's a leak in the air pressure tube leading to it (as described in section 2-2.) Replace the switch or tube.

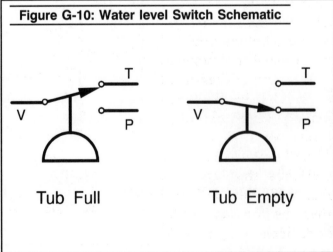

Figure G-10: Water level Switch Schematic

Tub Full   Tub Empty

2-6(c) TIMERS

The timer is the brain of the washer. It controls everything in the cycle. In addition to telling the motor when and which way to run, it tells any clutch solenoids when to engage, the fill valve when to open, dispenser solenoids when to open, etc.

Most washers still have mechanical, that is, motor-operated timers. Some newer machines have digital timers and control (computer) boards.

Diagnosing digital machines is often a matter of reading the digital fault code or performing a self test. Testing procedures and fault codes for individual models can usually be found on a paper located inside the console.

A mechanical timer is nothing more than a motor that drives a set of cams which open and close switches. Yet it is one of the most expensive parts in your washer, so don't be too quick to diagnose it as the problem. Usually the FIRST thing a layman looks at is the timer; it should be the LAST. And don't forget that timers are electrical parts, which are usually non-returnable. If you buy one, and it turns out *not* to be the problem, you've just wasted the money.

In a wiring diagram, a mechanical timer may appear in two different ways (Figure G-11). The wiring and switches that are inside the timer will either be drawn with dark lines, or there will be a shaded or dotted line drawn around the timer's internal wiring and switches.

DIAGNOSIS

If the timer is not advancing, well, that's pretty obvious. Replace the timer or timer drive motor, or have it rebuilt as described below.

Timers can be difficult to diagnose. The easiest way is to go through everything else in the system that's malfunctioning. If none of the other components are bad, then it may be the timer.

Remember that a timer is simply a set of on-off switches. The switches are turned off and on by a cam, which is driven by the timer motor. Timer wires are color-coded or number-coded.

Let's say you've got a spin solenoid problem that you think you've traced to your timer. First unplug the machine. Look at your wiring diagram and see which internal timer switch feeds the spin solenoid. (See figure G-12) In this case, the pink colored wire and the red

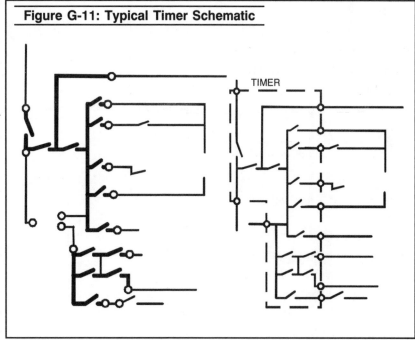

Figure G-11: Typical Timer Schematic

TIMER

colored wire with a white stripe lead to switch #10 inside the timer. REMOVE those wires from the timer and touch the test leads to those terminals. Make sure the timer is in the "on" position and slowly turn the timer all the way through a full cycle. (On some timers, you cannot turn the dial while it is on. Whirlpool Direct Drive models (chapter 4) are this way. You must simply test the timer one click at a time. Be patient!)

You should see continuity make and break at least once in the cycle; usually many times. If it doesn't, the internal contacts are bad; replace the timer.

A *special* timer problem occurs only in machines with direct-reversing motors. The Whirlpool Direct-Drive models (Chapter 4) are prone to this confusing problem, though it's not too terribly common. The symptoms are that when you open the lid at the end of the cycle,

the tub hasn't drained. You hear the motor running throughout the cycle, but it doesn't spin or drain; you may also notice that you hear it *agitating* when it's supposed to be *spinning*.

For the motor to reverse, the timer must interrupt power to it for a moment. When the timer gets worn, this simply doesn't happen. The motor doesn't get a chance to start in the opposite direction, so it continues to run in the same direction (agitate) until something interrupts the circuit and stops the motor. Like *you*, lifting the lid. You can see how the symptoms might appear to be intermittent and a bit confusing. The solution: replace the timer.

In general, timers cannot be rebuilt by the novice. Check with your parts dealer; if it *can* be rebuilt, he'll get it done for you. If it's a common one,

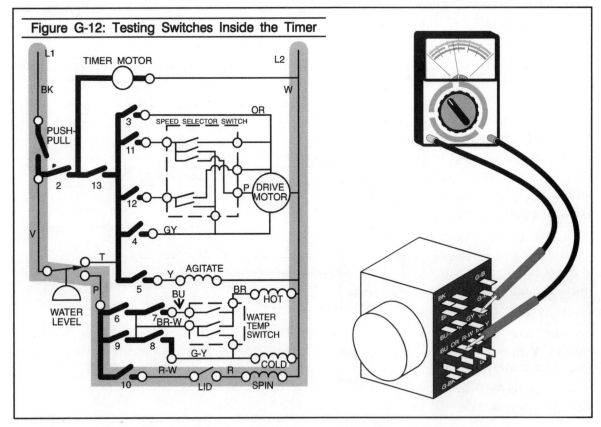

Figure G-12: Testing Switches Inside the Timer

your parts dealer may even have a re-built one in stock.

For the most part, if your timer is acting up, you need to replace it. To replace, mark the wires or note the color codes written on the timer. If you need to, you can draw a picture of the terminal arrangement and wire colors. If possible, change over the timer wires one-by-one; it can be easier. If there are any special wiring changes, they will be explained in instructions that come with the new timer.

2-6(d) SPEED SELECTOR AND WATER TEMPERATURE SWITCHES

The internal wiring for these switches is almost always shown with a shaded or dotted box around them (Figure G-13.)

The lettering inside the box will tell you what terminals to test. For example, with the temperature switch shown in figure G-13 set on "Warm wash, Cold rinse" all the switches marked with a "WC" will be closed. Take power off the machine, and remove all four wires from the switch. Test for continuity between the BU and the BR terminals; you should see good continuity. Test also between the BR-W and G-Y terminals. You should see good continuity.

Now test between the BR-W and BR terminals. There is no WC marking next to the middle switch, so the switch should be open. You should see *no* continuity with your VOM. Test the switch similarly for all settings.

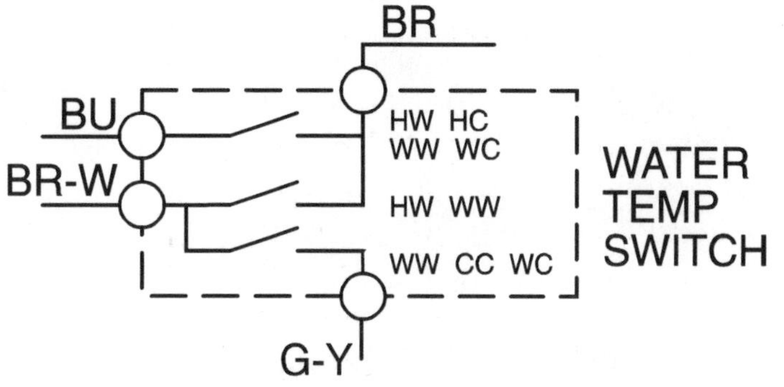

2-6(e) DRIVE MOTORS, START SWITCH, AND CAPACITORS

A motor that is trying to start, but can't for whatever reason, is using one heckuva lot of electricity. So much, in fact, that if it is allowed to continue being energized in a stalled state, it will start burning wires. To prevent this, an overload switch is installed on motors to cut power to them if they don't start within a certain amount of time.

If the motor is trying to start, but can't, you will hear certain things. First will be a click, followed immediately by a buzzing or "growling" sound. Then, after about 5 to 20 seconds of this sound, another click and the sound will stop. The sounds will keep repeating every minute or two. In some extreme cases, you may even smell burning.

If you hear the motor doing this, but it won't start, disconnect power and take all the load off it. For example, disconnect the drive belt, pump drive system, etc.

Try to start the motor again. If it still won't start, the motor, starting capacitor or speed selector switch is bad. (The speed selector switch may be trying to start the motor in two different speeds

Figure G-13: Typical Selector Switch

BR

BU

BR-W

HW HC
WW WC

HW WW

WW CC WC

G-Y

WATER TEMP SWITCH

at once.) If you have an ammeter, a stalled motor will be drawing 10 to 20 amps or more. Replace the bad component.

If the motor DOES start with the load removed, the pump or transmission may be locked up; See section 2-3 and 2-4(a).

CAPACITOR

Not all machines have external motor starting capacitors.

On machines that do, most external capacitors are mounted piggyback on the motor. (Figure G-14) Some direct-drive machines have their capacitors mounted separately behind the control console. See the chapter about *your* machine for details.

If your machine has an external capacitor, unplug the machine and DISCHARGE THE CAPACITOR. BE CAREFUL; IT CAN GIVE YOU A NASTY SHOCK, *EVEN IF THE WASHER IS NOT PLUGGED IN!* You can discharge it by shorting the two terminals on your capacitor with your screwdriver. Be careful not to touch the metal part of your screwdriver with your hands while you do this.

After discharging the capacitor, disconnect its leads and test it. Set your VOM on Rx1 and touch the two test probes to the two capacitor terminals. Initially, the meter should bounce towards the right of the scale (good continuity), then slowly move back to the left side a bit as the capacitor builds resistance. Reverse the two probes on the terminals. The meter reading should act the same way. If you do not get these readings, replace the capacitor.

STARTING SWITCH

Whirlpool machines have a *centrifugal* starting switch mounted piggyback on the motor. Testing the switch is most easily accomplished by replacing it.

Remember that starting switches are electrical parts, which are generally not returnable. If you test the switch by replacing it, and the problem turns out to be the motor itself, you will probably not be able to return the starting switch for a refund. But they're generally pretty cheap, and if it IS the problem, you just saved yourself the best part of a hundred bucks for a new motor.

MOTOR

If your motor is stalled (buzzing and/or tripping out on the overload switch) and the capacitor, starting switch and speed selector switches test O.K., the motor is bad. Replace it.

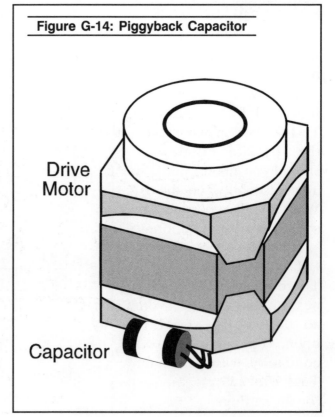

Figure G-14: Piggyback Capacitor

Drive Motor

Capacitor

Chapter 3

WHIRLPOOL / KENMORE BELT DRIVE

NOTE: Chapter 2 covers problems common to almost all washer designs. THIS chapter covers only diagnosis and repairs peculiar to Whirlpool-built machines. If you do not read Chapter 2 thoroughly before you read this chapter, you probably will not be able to properly diagnose your machine!!!!

The Whirlpool belt-driven design is well over thirty years old. The basic design has remained virtually unchanged in that time. Although it is extremely reliable, it does have its quirks. Fortunately, having been around for so long, the peculiarities of the design are pretty well known.

3-1 BASIC OPERATION

The design uses a single direction motor, with solenoids to engage and disengage the agitate and spin cycles and pump. (Figure W-1) The arrangement of control solenoids is peculiar to this design. It's called a "wigwag."

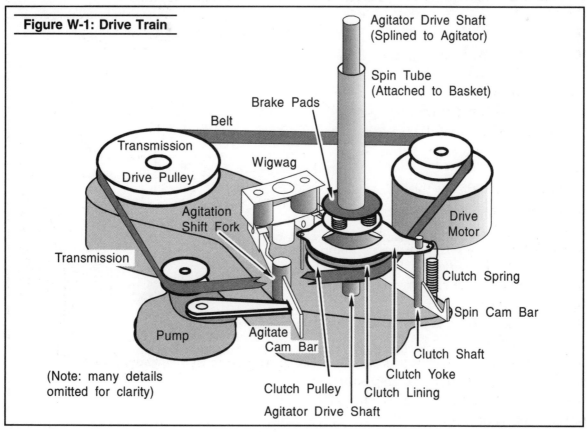

Figure W-1: Drive Train

Agitator Drive Shaft
(Splined to Agitator)

Spin Tube
(Attached to Basket)

Brake Pads

Belt

Transmission
Drive Pulley

Wigwag

Agitation
Shift Fork

Drive
Motor

Transmission

Clutch Spring

Spin Cam Bar

Pump

Agitate
Cam Bar

Clutch Shaft

Clutch Yoke

(Note: many details omitted for clarity)

Clutch Pulley

Clutch Lining

Agitator Drive Shaft

Whenever the motor is running, gears in the transmission keep the wigwag rotating back and forth in a motion similar to the agitator. Each solenoid's plunger is attached to a yoke with a pin through it. This pin rides in a slot in the cam bar (more about the cam bar later.)

When one of the solenoids is energized, the plunger retracts. The pin in the plunger rides in a different part of the cam bar slot than before. (Figure W-2) Since the wigwag is constantly moving back and forth, the pin will push the cam bar to a different position.

The pump turns in only one direction and has a flapper valve located within its housing. To change from recirculate to pumpout, the flapper valve changes position.

Figure W-2: Cam Bar Action

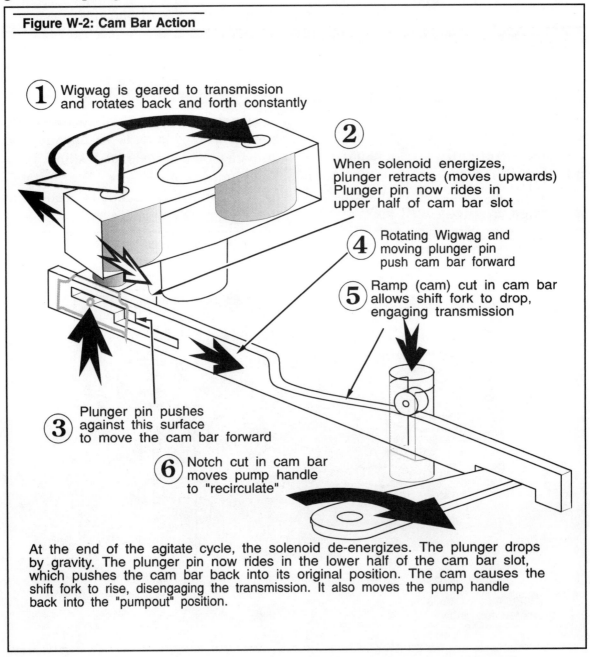

(1) Wigwag is geared to transmission and rotates back and forth constantly

(2) When solenoid energizes, plunger retracts (moves upwards) Plunger pin now rides in upper half of cam bar slot

(4) Rotating Wigwag and moving plunger pin push cam bar forward

(5) Ramp (cam) cut in cam bar allows shift fork to drop, engaging transmission

(3) Plunger pin pushes against this surface to move the cam bar forward

(6) Notch cut in cam bar moves pump handle to "recirculate"

At the end of the agitate cycle, the solenoid de-energizes. The plunger drops by gravity. The plunger pin now rides in the lower half of the cam bar slot, which pushes the cam bar back into its original position. The cam causes the shift fork to rise, disengaging the transmission. It also moves the pump handle back into the "pumpout" position.

AGITATE CYCLE

During the agitate cycle, the agitate solenoid (the solenoid on the right side of the wigwag, as you look into the back of the washer) energizes and pushes the agitate cam bar towards the front of the washer. (See Figures W-2 and W-3) The agitate cam bar does two things:

1) The ramp cut into its shape lets the agitator fork drop down towards the transmission. This engages the transmission and causes the agitator to agitate.

2) The pump lever moves, causing the pump to recirculate.

When the agitate cycle is over, power is removed from the solenoid, and the cam bar moves towards the back of the washer. This disengages the transmission and changes the pump back into the pumpout mode.

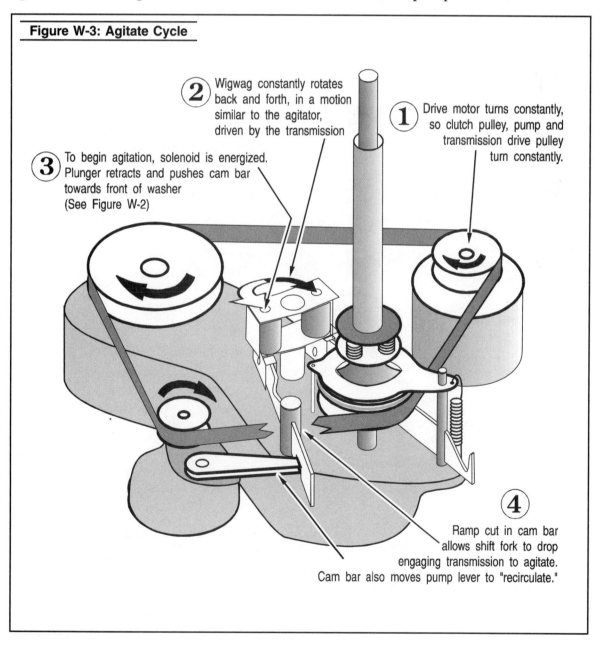

Figure W-3: Agitate Cycle

2) Wigwag constantly rotates back and forth, in a motion similar to the agitator, driven by the transmission

1) Drive motor turns constantly, so clutch pulley, pump and transmission drive pulley turn constantly.

3) To begin agitation, solenoid is energized. Plunger retracts and pushes cam bar towards front of washer (See Figure W-2)

4) Ramp cut in cam bar allows shift fork to drop engaging transmission to agitate. Cam bar also moves pump lever to "recirculate."

SPIN CYCLE

During the spin cycle, the spin solenoid energizes (the solenoid on the left side of the wigwag, as you look into the back of the washer.) The wigwag plunger pulls the spin cam bar towards the back of the washer. (See Figure W-4) This allows the clutch bar to drop, and the clutch spring and brake springs move the clutch yoke downward. The brake disengages and the clutch lining touches the clutch pulley. The clutch engages, and the basket starts spinning.

When the spin cycle is over, or when the washer lid is lifted, power is removed from the solenoid. The cam bar moves towards the front of the washer, pushing the clutch bar and yoke upwards. The clutch disengages and the brake engages, bringing the basket to a rapid stop.

This whole clutch and braking assembly is known as the basket drive assembly.

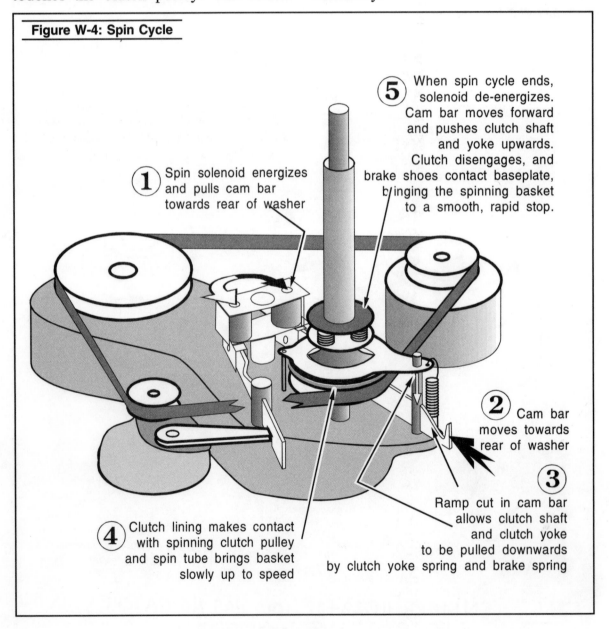

Figure W-4: Spin Cycle

1 Spin solenoid energizes and pulls cam bar towards rear of washer

5 When spin cycle ends, solenoid de-energizes. Cam bar moves forward and pushes clutch shaft and yoke upwards. Clutch disengages, and brake shoes contact baseplate, bringing the spinning basket to a smooth, rapid stop.

2 Cam bar moves towards rear of washer

3 Ramp cut in cam bar allows clutch shaft and clutch yoke to be pulled downwards by clutch yoke spring and brake spring

4 Clutch lining makes contact with spinning clutch pulley and spin tube brings basket slowly up to speed

3-2 OPENING THE CABINET AND CONSOLE

See figure W-5 for details about opening the cabinet and console.

In raising the lid of the washer, it is better to use a putty knife. You can use a thin-bladed screwdriver, but you might chip or scratch the paint.

A wiring diagram is usually pasted to the back of the machine.

3-3 WHAT TYPICALLY GOES WRONG WITH THESE MACHINES

Diagnosis begins by checking to see exactly which cycles the washer is missing or malfunctioning in. For example, if the washer won't drain or spin, check also to see if it will agitate before you empty the tub. In this type of washer, you can pretty well narrow down the cause just by knowing the exact symptoms.

Here are the most common complaints:

SYMPTOM: THE WASHER AGITATES BUT WON'T DRAIN OR SPIN.

In this design, the water level interlocks the spin cycle. The basket will only spin if the water is pumped almost all the way out. If the pump is not pumping out water, the washer will not begin to spin. Check for a kinked drain hose. Also check the pump as described in Section 3-10. Often there will be a strong burning smell along with this problem. This is almost always a locked pump; the burning smell comes from the stopped rubber belt riding on the turning motor pulley.

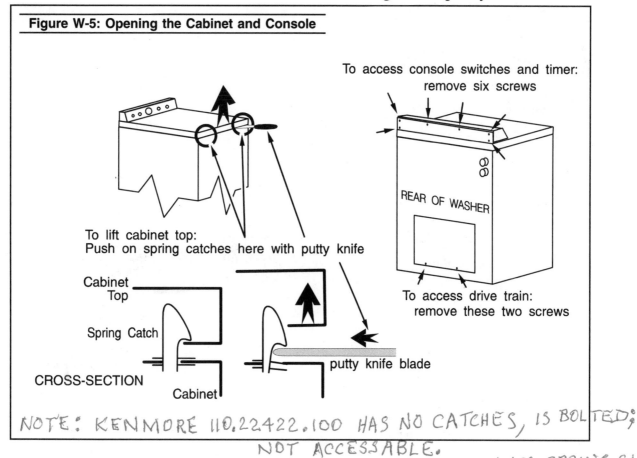

Figure W-5: Opening the Cabinet and Console

To access console switches and timer:
remove six screws

To lift cabinet top:
Push on spring catches here with putty knife

REAR OF WASHER

To access drive train:
remove these two screws

Cabinet Top

Spring Catch

CROSS-SECTION

Cabinet

putty knife blade

NOTE: KENMORE 110.22422.100 HAS NO CATCHES, IS BOLTED; NOT ACCESSABLE.
BACK PANEL IS SECURED AT BOTTOM WITH 2 SCREWS; SPRING CLIPS AT TOP. NOTE IF TOP EDGE GOES BEHIND CONSOLE BACK EDGE.
TO SECURE: SET SPRINGS INTO BACK PNL NOTCHES, VERIFY LIPS ENGAGE AT BOTTOM

SYMPTOM: THE WASHER AGITATES AND DRAINS BUT WON'T SPIN.
(Clothes are dripping wet at end of cycle.)

Something is interrupting either the electrical spin circuit or the mechanical spin mechanism.

The basket will not start spinning if the lid is up. A bad lid switch will have the same effect. Close the lid; if the basket still does not spin, check the lid switch for continuity. Also check to see that the switch striker is not broken off.

If this doesn't solve the problem, test for power at the left (spin) wigwag solenoid when in the spin cycle. The easiest way to do this is to unplug the washer and switch the red and yellow wigwag leads as shown in figure W-6. Plug the washer in and set it in the SPIN cycle. If it AGITATES, then you are getting power to the solenoid. Either the wigwag solenoid itself is bad, or the clutch is worn out.

Put the wires back on the correct terminals and watch the spin cam bar as you start the washer in "spin." If the spin cam bar does not move, the wigwag is bad; replace it as described in section 3-11. Check also for a broken pin in the plunger. If the spin cam bar DOES move, the clutch is worn out; see section 3-15.

If switching the wires does NOT cause the washer to agitate, then put the two leads back on the correct terminals and check the

following:

The water level is sensed by the water level switch. If the switch is bad, the washer will not spin. Test the switch as described in sections 3-4 and 2-6(b).

Often one of the wigwag wires will break, usually very near the wigwag itself. Furthermore, the break may be internal; you will see no damage on the outside of the wire. Test the wires for continuity and repair if bad.

The timer contacts may be bad. Test for continuity through the spin solenoid circuit of the timer as described in section 2-6(c). If there is no continuity, replace the timer as described in section 3-5.

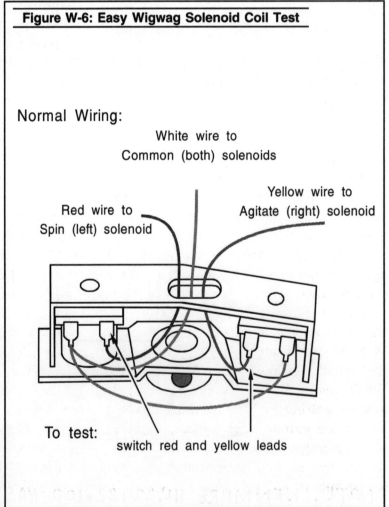

Figure W-6: Easy Wigwag Solenoid Coil Test

Normal Wiring:

White wire to
Common (both) solenoids

Red wire to
Spin (left) solenoid

Yellow wire to
Agitate (right) solenoid

To test: switch red and yellow leads

SET THE BOTTOM SCREW UNDER THE HOSES FIRST. IF UNABLE TO START EITHER SCREW, PRY SIDE PANEL OUT OF THE LIP 3" IN FROM BACK, PULL DOWN ON SOLENOIDS/PUT A SCREWDRIVER THR...

SYMPTOM: THE WASHER FILLS BUT WON'T AGITATE, DRAIN OR SPIN.

The belt is probably broken; replace as described in section 3-13.

If the motor hums, but does not turn, Check as described in section 2-6(e). If the motor turns with no load, check the drive pulley and pump pulley to see which is locked. If the motor doesn't start with no load, replace it as described in section 3-12.

If you don't even hear the motor hum, the motor, motor starting switch or capacitor may be bad; see section 3-12. Also check the motor circuits of the timer as described in section 2-6(c). Also check for a locked transmission as described in section 2-5(c). If the transmission is locked, see section 3-14.

SYMPTOM: THE WASHER WON'T AGITATE, BUT DOES FILL, DRAIN AND SPIN.

When you set the timer at the beginning of a wash cycle, the fill solenoid valve opens first. When the water level switch senses the correct water level, the solenoid valve closes, the motor starts, and the agitation (right) wigwag solenoid energizes.

Usually this problem is a burnt out agitation solenoid, but there are other possibilities.

To test the agitation solenoid, switch the wigwag leads as shown in Figure W-6. Make sure the tub is full and start the washer somewhere in the AGITATE cycle. If the basket SPINS, then you're getting power to the wigwag. Either the agitate wigwag coil is burnt or the plunger or pin is broken.

Another possibility is that the agitator spline is stripped, as described in section 3-13. If the washer agitates very

weakly, i.e. you can stop the agitator with your hands, this is a very strong possibility.

The last possibility is that the transmission is broken internally. See section 3-14.

NOTE: The lid switch is NOT interlocked with the agitate cycle in these machines; they WILL agitate with the lid up.

SYMPTOM: THE WASHER DOES ABSOLUTELY NOTHING; NO FILL, AGITATE, DRAIN OR SPIN.

Check for power to the machine.

Check the main power circuit through the timer; it may have bad contacts. See section 2-6(c).

Check the imbalance switch. (Kenmore models ONLY) See section 3-6.

SYMPTOM: THE WASHER IS VERY NOISY IN SPIN OR WHEN BRAKING.

The clutch or brake linings are probably badly worn. If so, replacing the basket drive will solve your noise problem. See section 3-15.

If the centerpost (spin tube) bearings are worn, replacing the basket drive will *not* solve your noise problem. You will need to call a *qualified* service technician to replace the bearings, or simply junk the washer. (I stress the word *qualified*, because it is a specialized job that many technicians will not tackle.)

The way to tell the difference is to listen to the noise the machine is making. If the machine is making a squealing or groaning noise, the problem is more likely to be the basket drive. If it is more like a rattling sound, the centerpost bearings are probably worn out.

A PANEL HOLE & PULL DOWN. WHEN BOTH SIDES ARE TIGHT-VERIFY THE END OF EACH SIDE GETS PRIED OVER THE LIP. (AGAINST THE SPRING)

A secondary check is to look at the clutch lining. On late models, there are three little pads riveted to the clutch plate. (Figure W-7) Older models had a full disc lining, rather than the three little pads. The lining touches the clutch pulley directly when the clutch is engaged. If it gets worn too badly, the rivets will screech against the clutch pulley. Take a look at the pads or lining. If it looks too thin, it's probably worn out. Also inspect the clutch surface on top of the pulley for any scoring or gouging. If there is any, your clutch is worn out. Replace the basket drive assembly as described in section 3-15.

SYMPTOM: THE WASHER LEAKS.

See section 2-4 on leaks and backed up drains.

On these machines, leaks usually come from the pump (section 3-10) or the air dome or other tub fitting (section 3-9.) Sometimes, there will be a leak in the fill hose, or in a bleach or softener dispenser.

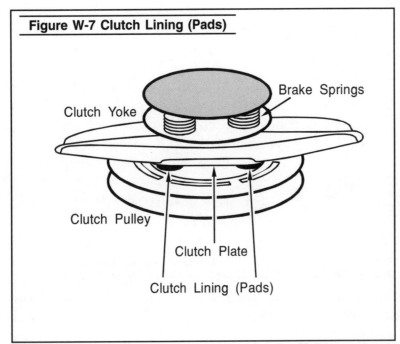

Figure W-7 Clutch Lining (Pads)

Clutch Yoke

Brake Springs

Clutch Pulley

Clutch Plate

Clutch Lining (Pads)

SYMPTOM: EXCESSIVE VIBRATION WHEN SPINNING.

If redistributing the clothes doesn't seem to help, see Section 3-7 on replacing the snubber and cleaning the snubber pad.

INTERMITTENT SYMPTOMS.

Usually, with intermittent problems, you simply must know the system and just look at things until you see something malfunctioning.

Some intermittent problems may be traceable to electrical problems, such as a loose terminal or worn wire. However, most intermittent problems with these machines come from mechanical causes.

For example, if the belt is loose, the machine may not spin sometimes, may not pump out at other times, and still other times it may not agitate. The solution is obviously to tighten the belt (or replace it if it is badly worn.)

Another aggravating and difficult to diagnose symptom is caused by worn cam bars. The washer may appear to slip in and out of the spin cycle at very short intervals. Or it may start spinning and suddenly stop, then restart a minute later.

If the washer tries to spin and agitate at the same time, it usually means that the spin plunger is bent, or the spin cam bar is badly worn.

There is also a very stiff leaf spring that holds the cam bars down in place (Figure W-8.) The bolt that holds this leaf spring in place has been known to back out, or the spring can break, causing all sorts of strange symptoms. The bolt can be replaced without removing the transmission, but it's a real bear of a job.

3-4 WATER LEVEL SWITCH

The water level switch is located in the control panel on top of the cabinet. For access to the switch, see section 3-2. Test the switch as described in section 2-6(b), using figure W-9. If the water level switch is bad, replace it.

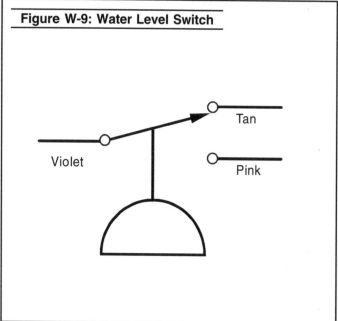

Figure W-9: Water Level Switch

Violet — Tan — Pink

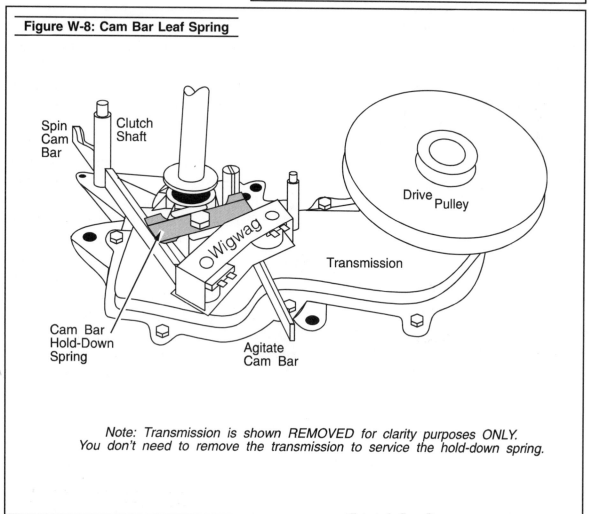

Figure W-8: Cam Bar Leaf Spring

Spin Cam Bar / Clutch Shaft / Wigwag / Drive Pulley / Transmission / Cam Bar Hold-Down Spring / Agitate Cam Bar

Note: Transmission is shown REMOVED for clarity purposes ONLY. You don't need to remove the transmission to service the hold-down spring.

3-5 TIMER

Test the timer as described in section 2-6(c).

Two types of timers were used: standard frame and quick-disconnect. (See Figure W-10)

To replace a defective timer, first unplug the washer. Pull the knob out, hold the timer dial and turn the timer knob to the left to unscrew it. (Figure W-10)

The standard frame timer has a locknut that holds the timer dial on and six splines that keep it in place on the timer shaft. When re-installing the dial, you must get it in the right part of the cycle. It can only go on the shaft in six differ-

ent ways. If you've replaced the timer, you just have play with the dial until you get on the right way.

The quick-disconnect has a D-shaped shaft that the timer dial just slips onto.

Remove the locknut, if necessary, and remove the timer dial. Remove the two timer mounting screws from the front of the console. If you have a standard frame timer, mark the timer wires before removing them, so you can get them on the correct terminals of the new timer. Better yet, if you can remove the wires from the old timer and put them directly on the new timer, one by one, it can be faster and easier.

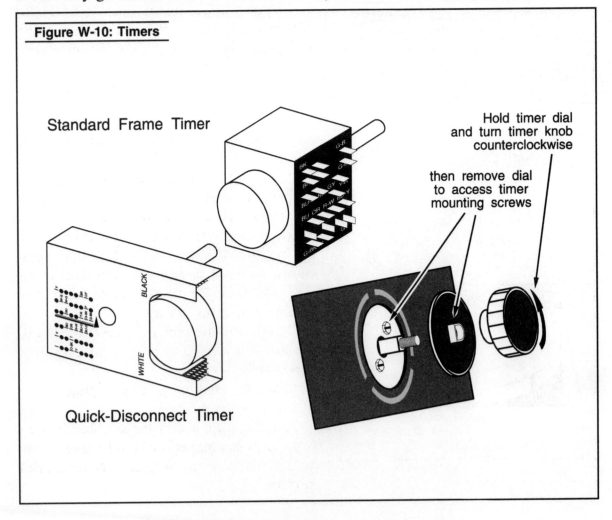

Figure W-10: Timers

Standard Frame Timer

Hold timer dial
and turn timer knob
counterclockwise

then remove dial
to access timer
mounting screws

Quick-Disconnect Timer

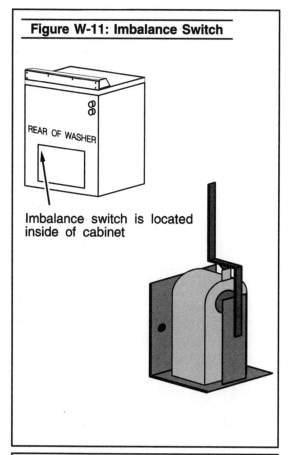

Figure W-11: Imbalance Switch

REAR OF WASHER

Imbalance switch is located inside of cabinet

3-6 IMBALANCE SWITCH
(Kenmore only)

In SOME Kenmore models only, there is an imbalance switch mounted inside the cabinet (on the left side, as you look at it from the back.)(Figure W-11.) If the load is not balanced, the base plate (to which the tub is attached) will move around until it contacts the imbalance switch. The motor will cut off and a buzzer will sound. The buzzer is built into the imbalance switch.

Usually, when they go bad, the washer will intermittently cut out for no apparent reason. You may also see a bright flash; this is the switch arcing. Sometimes, the switch may burn out altogether and it will seem as if the machine isn't getting any power at all. This switch is easy to replace; just remember to unplug the machine first.

3-7 SNUBBER AND SNUBBER PAD

If the washer vibrates too badly, and redistributing the clothes doesn't seem to help, it could be that the snubber spring is broken, or that the snubber block or pad is choked up with soap.

Unplug the washer and raise the lid.

The snubber is in the right rear corner of the washer. (Figure W-12) Lift the spring (there's a lot of tension on it) to remove the snubber block. Be careful not to catch your fingers under the spring!

To remove the spring, remove the single nut and bolt that hold it in place, and twist it out of its mounts.

Clean the snubber pad by wiping it with a wet towel or sponge.

Roughen the face of the snubber block a little with sandpaper, or simply take it outside and rub it on the sidewalk or a brick surface.

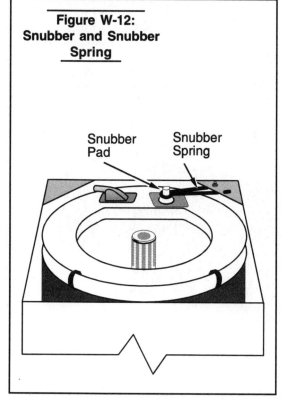

**Figure W-12:
Snubber and Snubber
Spring**

Snubber
Pad

Snubber
Spring

3-8 AGITATOR REPLACEMENT

Your agitator is splined to the transmission driveshaft, and secured with a stud. Access to the stud is in one of two ways. (Figure W-13) Some have a removable plastic cap on top; you simply pry it off with a screwdriver, and you will see the stud with a nut on it. In others, a one-piece threaded cap is screwed directly to the stud itself. To remove the threaded cap or nut, hold the agitator (this will keep the driveshaft from turning) and unscrew.

But what if the agitator splines are stripped? You can hold the agitator all you want, and the shaft will keep turning with the nut or the threaded cap.

Here's a good confirmation of a stripped spline. Put the timer in an agitate cycle. Let the washer fill and begin to agitate. If you can hold the agitator still, and the nut or cap is reciprocating back and forth, the spline is probably stripped.

Here's a little trick to get the nut or cap off when you can't hold the shaft still; let the *machinery* hold it still *for* you.

If you have a nut & stud, hit the nut with a little WD-40 and put a ratchet on it. Make sure the ratchet is set for the proper direction; to *remove* the nut. Hold the rachet and start your washer in the agitation cycle. The nut will back off with each sweep of the agitator shaft.

If you have a threaded cap, you can do the same thing by hand. Simply start the machine in the agitate cycle and turn the cap counterclockwise.

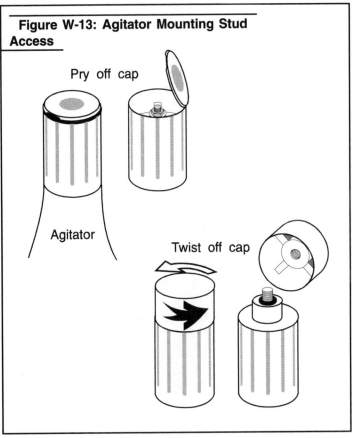

Figure W-13: Agitator Mounting Stud Access

Pry off cap

Agitator

Twist off cap

3-9 BASKET REMOVAL AND TUB FITTINGS

To replace any leaking tub fittings, you must remove the basket.

Unplug the washer and raise the cabinet top as described in section 3-2.

Remove the agitator as described in section 3-8.

Remove the snubber spring as described in section 3-7.

Remove the water inlet fitting from the tub ring. (Figure W-14)

Carefully note the sizes and positions of the tub ring clips as you remove them.(Figure W-14.

Remove the spanner nut. (Figure W-15) A special tool is available from your appliance parts dealer. The tool is a very common item and thus is pretty cheap.

Figure W-14: Tub Ring Area

VIEW:
Top of Tub,
with Cabinet Top raised

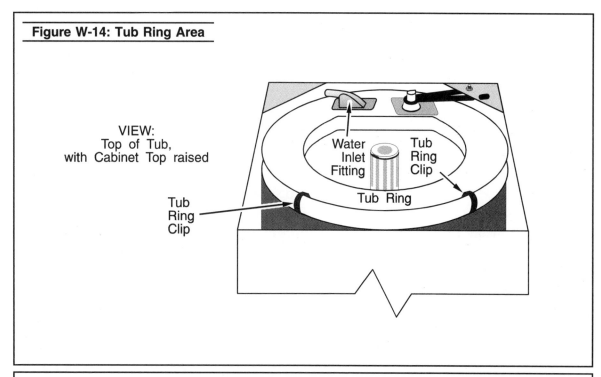

Figure W-15: Spanner Nut

The Spanner Nut connects
the Basket to the Drive Block
(See Figure W-23)
and compresses the drive block
around the spin tube

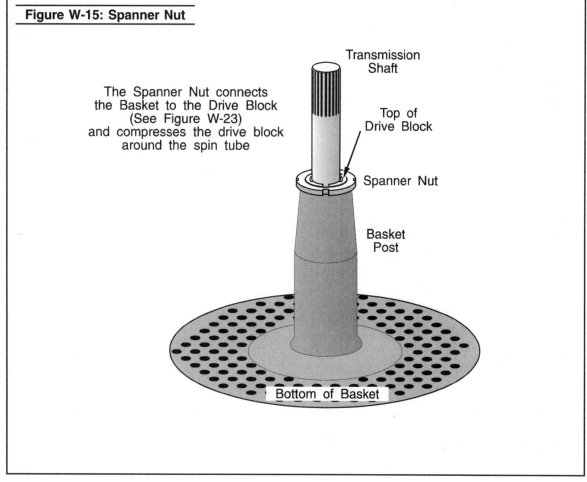

Lift the basket straight up and out.

INSTALLATION is basically the opposite of removal.

Most of the tub fittings have rubber seals and locking nuts or rings. Simply twist the ring counterclockwise to remove.

The air dome is the fitting that attaches the water pressure switch hose to the tub. It is a common source of leaks. To remove the dome, remove the hose from it and turn it 90 degrees to unlock it from the seal.

3-10 PUMPS

In this design, the basket will not start spinning until almost all the water is pumped out of the tub.

Whirlpool washers were equipped, at various times, with three different pumps. (Figure W-16) In the parts houses, they are commonly known as two-hose, three-hose, and four-hose pumps, for obvious reasons. Whirlpool pumps cannot be rebuilt; they must be replaced. Fortunately, they're very common items, so they are pretty cheap.

REMOVAL

Drain the tub. Remove the back panel of the washer. Loosen the motor mounting bolts and remove tension from the belt.

Lean the washer back against the wall, following the safety tips in section 1-4. Put a bucket underneath the pump and remove the hoses. Pull out the two mounting bolts and remove the pump. Rocking the pump away from the drive belt will help disengage the belt, and also the pump lever from the cam bar. DO NOT MOVE THE PUMP LEVER YET.

Check the belt for wear as described in section 2-5(a), especially for burned or glazed spots where it rode over the locked pump pulley or motor drive pulley. Replace the belt if it is worn, following the instructions in section 3-13.

INSTALLATION

Set the pump lever in the same position as the pump that came out. Rock the pump in place, the same way as you pulled the old one out. Make sure the pump lever goes into the slot in the agitate cam bar, and install the mounting bolts. Tension the belt as described in section 3-13.

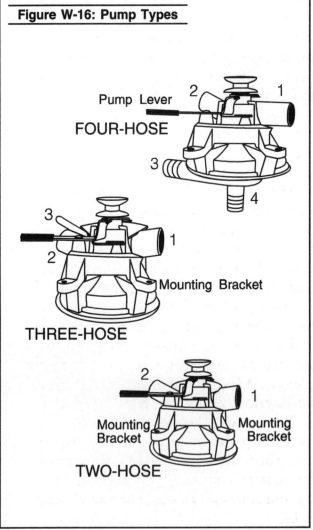

Figure W-16: Pump Types

3-11 WIGWAG AND CAM BARS

The wigwag is located inside the back panel of the machine. Replacement is fairly easy. First, take all power off the machine. Note which color wires go to which wigwag terminals and remove the wires. Loosen the wigwag setscrew and pull the wigwag straight off the shaft. Replace the wigwag directly, taking care to get the right wires on the right terminals. Also make sure that the plungers fit loosely in the wigwag so that they can move freely. Replace the setscrew, making sure it goes in the hole on the wigwag drive shaft, and tighten securely.

Normally, you will not need to replace the plungers, even when you replace the wigwag. If you see that one is bent or the pin is badly worn, replace the plunger.

The plungers can be quite difficult to replace. The pins that connect them to the cam bars are hardened and thus difficult to cut through.

The first step is to remove power from the machine and cut through the pin. Use a hacksaw blade, diagonals or bolt cutters. Clearance is tight. Sometimes it's easier to hacksaw through the body of the yoke than to cut the pin.

Once you've cut through the pin, remove the wigwag as described above and replace the plunger, using the instructions that come with the new plunger. Make sure you install the plastic insert. It keeps the machine quieter.

To replace the spin cam bar, you must drop the transmission slightly as described in section 3-13. To replace the agitate cam bar, you must remove the transmission as described in section 3-14.

3-12 DRIVE MOTOR

Single speed, two-speed and three-speed motors were used at different times in these washers. The different motors were, at times, produced by different manufacturers. When you're replacing a motor, capacitor or motor starting switch, you'll need either numbers off the motor or switch you're replacing, or a model number for the washer, to make sure you get the right parts.

NOTE: On two-and three-speed machines (Those that have a "permanent press" setting on the timer dial) a timer failure was usually the cause of a motor failure. If you replace the motor in one of these machines, you must replace the timer, too.

TESTING

Some of these machines have external capacitors mounted either piggyback on the motor or just inside the left side of the cabinet (as you look at the back of the washer.) If yours does, DISCHARGE IT and test it as described in section 2-6(e) before doing any work on the motor.

Now test the start switch as described in section 2-6(e).

If your capacitor and motor starting switch test O.K., replace the drive motor. It is held in place by two mounting nuts.

3-13 DRIVE BELT

Open the back of the machine and inspect the belt as described in section 2-5(a).

If the belt is broken, make sure you check the pump and transmission pulleys to see if they are locked. This may be the cause of the belt breaking.

REPLACING THE BELT

Unfortunately, the belt is not easy to replace on this machine. To get the belt past the clutch shaft, you actually have to drop the transmission out slightly, and sometimes the transmission needs to be realigned afterwards. Here are the steps:

1) Prepare the machine: Unplug it, siphon out any water, and lay it down on its front side using the safety instructions in section 1-4(4). Remove the back panel.

2) Remove the clutch yoke spring, (Figure W-17)

3) Remove the braces and pump mounting bolts (Figure W-18)

4) Remove the lower left transmission mounting bolt. That is the mounting bolt next to the clutch shaft. Make sure you save the spacer that falls out.

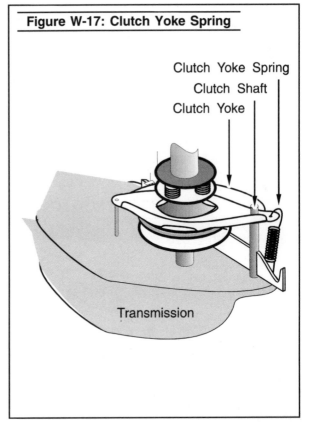

Figure W-17: Clutch Yoke Spring

Clutch Yoke Spring
Clutch Shaft
Clutch Yoke

Transmission

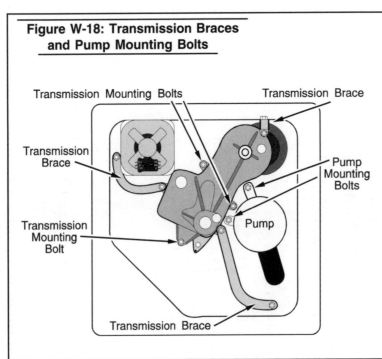

Figure W-18: Transmission Braces and Pump Mounting Bolts

Transmission Mounting Bolts
Transmission Brace
Transmission Brace
Pump Mounting Bolts
Transmission Mounting Bolt
Pump
Transmission Brace

5) You must bottom out the clutch shaft. Hold the wigwag's "spin" plunger up and tap the spin cam bar towards the back of the machine. The clutch shaft will drop down towards the bottom of the machine. (Figure W-19)

6) Loosen the two other transmission mounting bolts about 7 full turns. Then pull the transmission straight out until it stops against the bolts.

7) Remove the belt. If you have trouble getting it over the clutch shaft, back out the transmission mounting bolts another turn or two.

Figure W-19: Bottoming the Clutch Shaft

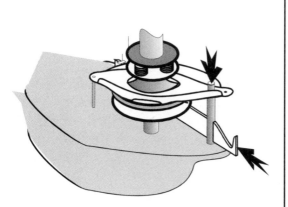

Tap Cam Bar Back
So That The Clutch Shaft Drops Down
As Far As It Will Go

INSTALLING THE BELT

Installation is basically the opposite of removal, except for the following:

1) Look at the transmission shaft, right where it comes out of the transmission and goes up into the basket drive. On most models, you will see a plastic "T"-bearing. (Figure W-20) This "T"-bearing is connected to the shaft by a ball; the ball fits in a hole in the shaft and a slot in the "T"-bearing. Make sure the ball is in the hole in the transmission shaft, and that the slot in the "T"-bearing fits down over the ball, before you tighten the transmission mounting bolts.

NOTE: Some models used a "C"-clip rather than a ball to hold the "T"-bearing in place. If you have one of these, ignore this step.

Figure W-20: "T"-Bearing

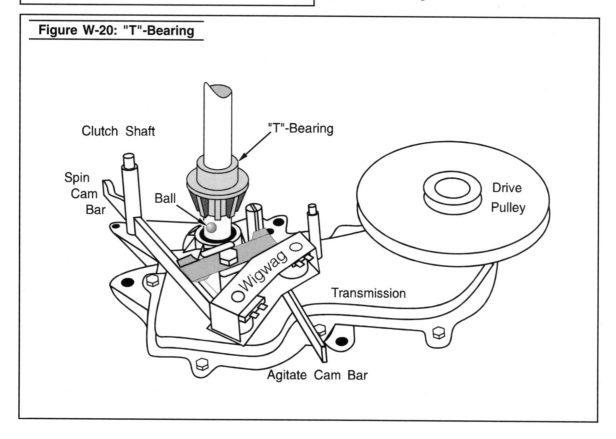

Clutch Shaft

"T"-Bearing

Spin
Cam
Bar

Ball

Wigwag

Drive
Pulley

Transmission

Agitate Cam Bar

2) The top of the clutch shaft has either two washers or a hex nut on it. Make sure these are replaced before you bolt the transmission back into place.

3) Make sure you replace the spacer before installing the lower left mounting bolt.

4) To set the correct tension on the belt, loosen the motor mounts and move the motor by hand. DO NOT use a lever or pry bar to set tension. The belt should deflect about 1/2" by hand, with easy pressure. (6 lbs is the official number, though there's no real practical way to measure it)

If the belt has never been adjusted before replacement, the new belt will probably not require adjusting. Make sure that the belt rides over all four pulleys: the pump pulley, the transmission drive pulley, the motor pulley and the clutch pulley.

5) You *may* get the machine all back together and find that the spin cycle has problems. The machine may not spin at all, or it may spin very slowly. If so, the transmission needs to be aligned. This is a tricky procedure, so be careful:

Remove the three braces from the transmission. Back off your three transmission mounting bolts about 1/2 to 1 turn; just enough so the transmission will drift a little. The transmission should be just slightly loose, and all three bolts must be backed out the same amount.

Set your washer upright and level. Make sure there is no water or clothes in the basket, and START THE WASHER IN THE SPIN CYCLE. Let it get up to speed, then stop the washer.

Unplug it. Without moving the washer, tighten the three transmission mounting bolts beneath it as evenly as possible. Test the machine to see that it still spins properly. If not, repeat the procedure. When you have it spinning properly, replace the three braces.

3-14 TRANSMISSION

If the transmission locks up, you will need to replace it; don't try to rebuild it yourself. They are pretty standard items; most appliance parts dealers carry rebuilt Whirlpool transmissions in stock. Make sure you bring the old transmission with you; they will need to match shaft lengths and there will probably be an exchange or a core charge.

To replace the transmission, follow the same instructions as in section 3-13, with the following additional steps:

1) Remove the agitator, as described in section 3-8.

2) Mark and remove the wigwag wires.

3) Remove the mounting bolts all the way.

4) Snap the yoke retainer out of the plastic clip on the clutch yoke (NOTE: some models used a spring clip rather than a plastic snap arrangement.) (Figure W-21)

5) Pull the transmission straight out.

When you get the transmission out, exchange all the old parts: cam bars and spring, clutch shaft, wigwag, "T"-bearing and ball, and the transmission drive

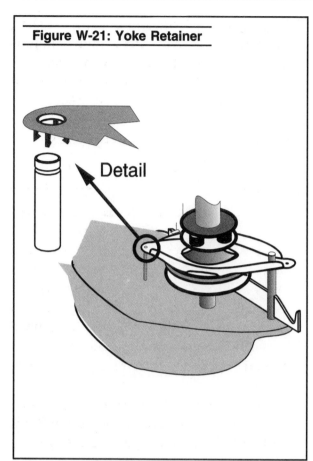

Figure W-21: Yoke Retainer

Detail

pulley. If you wish, you can replace the cam bars, T-bearing and ball as insurance against future problems. Two points to remember in exchanging the parts:

1) The drive pulley is originally assembled with a drop of glue on the setscrew threads. You may need to heat the hub of the drive pulley with a torch to get the setscrew out.

2) To get the agitator cam bar out, you will need to lift the agitator shaft. The easiest way to do this is to remove the "T"-bearing ball and pry the shaft upwards with a screwdriver, as shown in Figure W-22.

Installation is basically the opposite of removal. Make sure you read "INSTALLING THE BELT" in section 3-13.

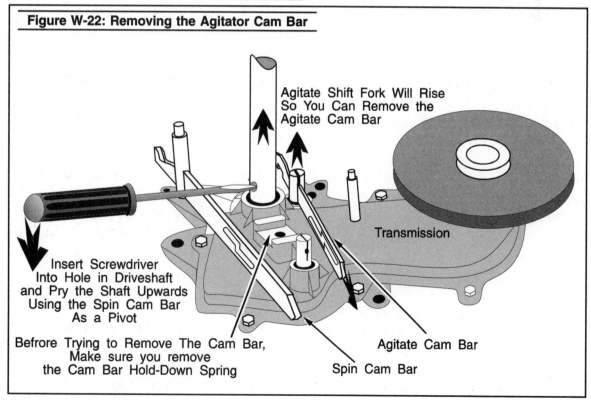

Figure W-22: Removing the Agitator Cam Bar

Agitate Shift Fork Will Rise So You Can Remove the Agitate Cam Bar

Transmission

Insert Screwdriver Into Hole in Driveshaft and Pry the Shaft Upwards Using the Spin Cam Bar As a Pivot

Befrore Trying to Remove The Cam Bar, Make sure you remove the Cam Bar Hold-Down Spring

Spin Cam Bar

Agitate Cam Bar

3-15 BASKET DRIVE

You cannot service the basket drive assembly, but you can replace it if the clutch or brake pads are worn. The basket drive assembly is not too terribly expensive.

To remove the basket drive assembly:

1) Remove the agitator as described in section 3-8.

2) Remove the basket as described in section 3-9.

3) Remove the drive block by tapping on the underside of it with a small hammer. (Figure W-23)

NOTE: *The metal of the drive block is pretty soft, so don't hit it too hard--just tap it. Also be careful not to hit the tub, or you may chip the porcelain interior.*

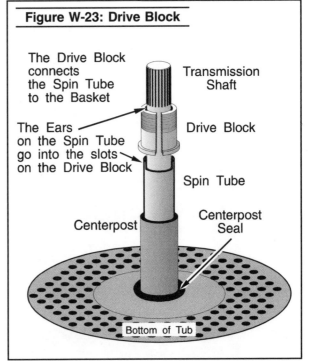

Figure W-23: Drive Block

The Drive Block connects the Spin Tube to the Basket

The Ears on the Spin Tube go into the slots on the Drive Block

Transmission Shaft

Drive Block

Spin Tube

Centerpost

Centerpost Seal

Bottom of Tub

4) Remove the transmission as described in section 3-14.

5) Pull the whole basket drive assembly straight out. Be careful not to damage the lower seal. (Figure W-24) If the lower seal pulls out with the basket drive, there is a special grease you can put in it. Ask your appliance parts dealer for some. Put the grease in the groove of the seal and put the seal back in place, groove side up.

Installation is basically the opposite of removal. However, note the following:

1) Put the basket drive in slowly so you don't damage any of the seals or bearings that it has to pass through in the centerpost.

2) Make sure that the tabs on the top of the spin tube fit in the notches in the drive block.

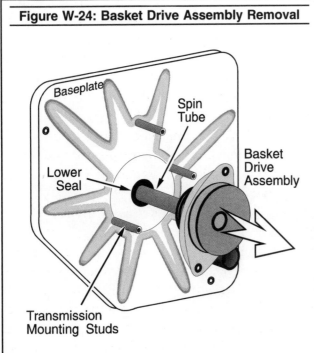

Figure W-24: Basket Drive Assembly Removal

Baseplate

Spin Tube

Lower Seal

Basket Drive Assembly

Transmission Mounting Studs

Chapter 4

WHIRLPOOL / KENMORE DIRECT DRIVE

NOTE: Chapter 2 covers problems common to both washer designs. THIS chapter covers only diagnosis and repairs peculiar to direct drive machines. If you do not read Chapter 2 thoroughly before you read this chapter, you probably will not be able to properly diagnose your machine!!!!

In the early 80's, Whirlpool completely redesigned their standard washing machine model. The result is the "Design 2000" series, known in the parts houses as "Whirlpool direct drive" models.

The most obvious feature of the design is that it does away with all drive belts. The motor is coupled directly to the transmission and pump. Other major changes include a new pedestal tub mounting system, a plastic tub with integral tub fittings, a liquid-ring basket balancing mechanism, and a mechanically direct-reversing transmission. Also, most of the component parts of the washer are held in place by spring clips or just a few screws, making them easy to replace.

4-1 BASIC SYSTEM (Figure DD-1)

This design uses a direct-reversing motor. In various models, single-speed, two-speed and three-speed motors were used.

A pump is mounted directly on the motor by spring clips. The pump moves water only during the spin cycle; during agitate, it is turning but it does not circulate water.

The motor is coupled directly to the transmission through a plastic and rubber flexible coupling.

Both the pump hub and transmission coupling will break away in the event of a pump or transmission lockup, preventing damage to the motor.

A clutch drum and shoes (mounted atop the transmission) allow the basket to come up to speed slowly during the spin cycle. The clutch drum rotates and is driven by gears inside the transmission. Similarly, a set of brake shoes (attached to the spin tube) contact a drum (attached to the bottom of the mounting pedestal) to provide a basket braking action to the tub whenever the washer is NOT in the spin cycle.

Changing between the agitate and spin cycles is accomplished mechanically within the transmission when the motor reverses.

In buying transmission and clutch parts for these machines, you may come across the term "neutral drain." Early versions of these machines began spinning with water still in the tub, so-called "direct spin" machines. A redesign created a "neutral drain" machine, where the tub would start draining before spin occurred.

4-2 OPENING THE CABINET AND CONSOLE

To service the timer or other electrical controls, remove the two screws from the base of the control console as shown in Figure DD-2.

In order to service just about anything else in the washer, you must re-move the whole cabinet as shown in Figure DD-2. If you need more space when performing a particular operation, you can twist the tab in the bottom center of the back of the cabinet. This will allow the back panel to drop away from the washer a little.

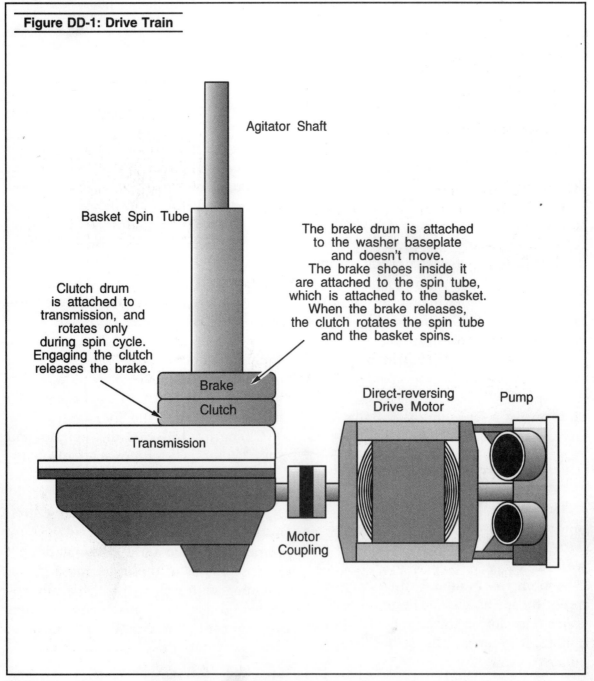

Figure DD-1: Drive Train

Agitator Shaft

Basket Spin Tube

The brake drum is attached to the washer baseplate and doesn't move. The brake shoes inside it are attached to the spin tube, which is attached to the basket. When the brake releases, the clutch rotates the spin tube and the basket spins.

Clutch drum is attached to transmission, and rotates only during spin cycle. Engaging the clutch releases the brake.

Brake

Clutch

Transmission

Direct-reversing Drive Motor

Pump

Motor Coupling

To change the transmission, you will need to remove the bottom panel as shown in Figure DD-2.

It *is* possible to service the pump and motor by removing the bottom panel only, but I do not recommend it. Space is tight and it can be very difficult. The pump is especially difficult; getting the hose clamps on and off can be a real son-of-a-gun. Better to just remove the cabinet; it's not difficult at all.

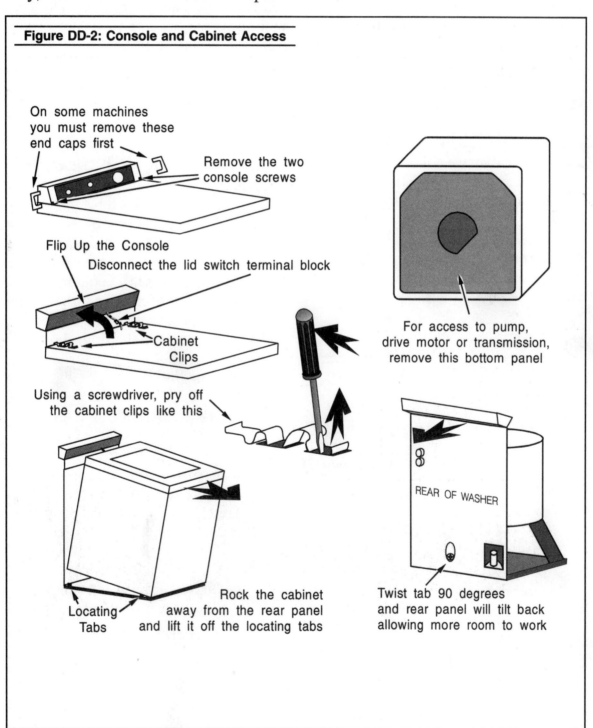

Figure DD-2: Console and Cabinet Access

On some machines you must remove these end caps first

Remove the two console screws

Flip Up the Console

Disconnect the lid switch terminal block

Cabinet Clips

Using a screwdriver, pry off the cabinet clips like this

For access to pump, drive motor or transmission, remove this bottom panel

REAR OF WASHER

Locating Tabs

Rock the cabinet away from the rear panel and lift it off the locating tabs

Twist tab 90 degrees and rear panel will tilt back allowing more room to work

4-3 WHAT TYPICALLY GOES WRONG WITH THESE MACHINES

After removing the cabinet, the machine can be started for testing by jumpering the lid switch leads. As always, when operating the machine without the cabinet, be careful not to touch any live electrical or moving parts.

SYMPTOM: NOISY OPERATION

A grinding noise during the agitate or spin cycle *may* mean that the motor coupling is damaged, but usually it is coming from the transmission. If so, replace the transmission. (Sections 4-8 & 4-9).

SYMPTOM: LEAKS

Any leaks are likely to be coming from one of three places:

1) The pump. See section 4-4.

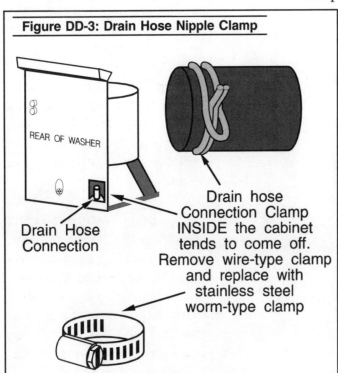

Figure DD-3: Drain Hose Nipple Clamp

REAR OF WASHER

Drain Hose Connection

Drain hose Connection Clamp INSIDE the cabinet tends to come off. Remove wire-type clamp and replace with stainless steel worm-type clamp

2) Early models had a small problem with the drain hose nipple (where the drain hose attaches to the back of the washer.) It used a spring-type hose clamp, which was prone to coming off. (Figure DD-3) Remove the clamp and replace it with a regular stainless steel worm-type clamp.

3) The centerpost seal can leak. Look for water coming from underneath the center of the tub. To replace, see section 4-7.

SYMPTOM: TUB NOT DRAINING

If the motor is turning, but the water will not drain from the tub, replace the pump as described in section 4-4. Often the pump has failed because the impeller has disintegrated, so make sure that you clear the hoses (especially the drain hose) when changing the pump Sometimes the check valve comes off the pump, and clogs the drain hose..

If the motor is not turning, see section 4-8.

SYMPTOM: NOT AGITATING AND / OR SPINNING

Check the usual things, i.e. main power, timer, switches, etc. as described in sections 2-6(a) thru (e). There is an unusual timer problem that sometimes pops up in these machines; see section 2-6(c).

The red wire in the motor harness is known for breaking inside the harness, where you can not see it. To test, pull gently on the red motor harness wire (don't yank it TOO hard!) If it comes off, you need to reconnect it or get a new wiring harness.

If spin is O.K. but the washer is not agitating, check for a stripped agitator spline or dogs as described in section 4-5.

Likewise, if the "ears" of the transmission spin tube have been known to break off; the symptom will be no spin.

If the motor is not turning, see section 4-8.

If the motor is turning, remove the motor as described in section 4-8 and check the transmission coupling. If it is badly damaged or destroyed, the transmission has locked up. See section 4-9.

If the motor is turning, and the transmission coupling looks okay, the transmission may be broken internally, or the clutch or brake may be malfunctioning. Remove the transmission as described in section 4-9 and check both the springs and linings on the clutch and brake. If the springs are broken or the linings are worn, replace as described in section 4-10. Usually there will be a squealing noise associated with worn clutch or brake shoes.

If the clutch and brake are O.K., try turning the transmission input shaft by hand. Turn in both directions and see if the agitator shaft and clutch drum are doing anything. If not, something has broken inside the transmission. Replace it.

SYMPTOM: TUB WON'T BALANCE (Even after you redistribute the clothes)

See section 4-6. Also look to see if any of the suspension springs mentioned in section 4-7 are broken.

4-4 PUMP

To get to the pump, remove the cabinet as described in section 4-2.

Have a bucket standing by to catch any left over water in the pump hoses, and remove them from the pump. The pump is held on to the motor by two spring clips. (Figure DD-4) Remove the spring clips and pull the pump off the motor shaft.

When replacing the pump, make sure you check the pump discharge hose for any impeller pieces that may be clogging it. Also, when installing the hose clamps, put them in a position where they won't hit the cabinet when the machine wobbles off-balance.

Figure DD-4: Pump Mount

To remove pump, remove the two spring clips

Drive Motor

Pump

4-5 AGITATOR

The agitator is held to the driveshaft by a bolt. To get to it, remove any softener dispenser by pulling it straight off. Remove the agitator cap by pulling or prying off with a screwdriver (depending on what kind you have; see Figure DD-5.) Remove the center bolt and tug straight up on the agitator skirt to remove. If you have trouble removing the bolt, see section 3-8 in Chapter 3.

Inspect the spline of the shaft and the agitator for wear. If the agitator is slipping on the agitator driveshaft spline, replace it.

4-6 BASKET SERVICE

The direct drive washer uses a liquid balancing system built into the basket. Around the top of the basket is a "ballast" compartment which is filled with a special liquid. When the basket spins,

Figure DD-6: Tub Ring

Remove bleach hose before removing tub ring

Tub Ring

Tub

To remove Tub Ring, push down on ring and release catches

the liquid inside this compartment moves around to dampen any imbalance present. Remove the basket to inspect this ballast compartment.

Removal of the basket requires a special spanner tool, available inexpensively from your parts dealer.

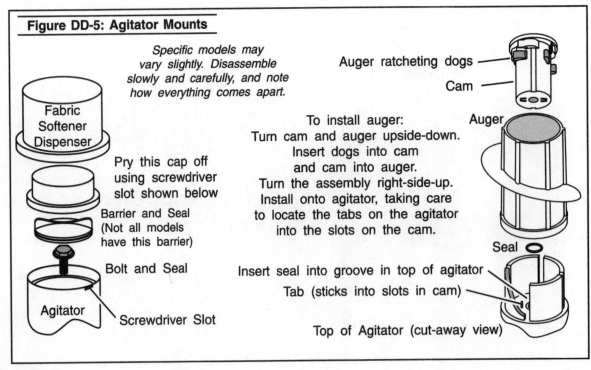

Figure DD-5: Agitator Mounts

Specific models may vary slightly. Disassemble slowly and carefully, and note how everything comes apart.

Fabric Softener Dispenser

Pry this cap off using screwdriver slot shown below

Barrier and Seal (Not all models have this barrier)

Bolt and Seal

Agitator

Screwdriver Slot

Auger ratcheting dogs

Cam

Auger

To install auger:
Turn cam and auger upside-down.
Insert dogs into cam and cam into auger.
Turn the assembly right-side-up.
Install onto agitator, taking care to locate the tabs on the agitator into the slots on the cam.

Seal

Insert seal into groove in top of agitator
Tab (sticks into slots in cam)

Top of Agitator (cut-away view)

First, remove the tub ring from the top of the tub (Figure DD-6) and the agitator (Section 4-5.)

Next, remove the fill line vacuum break by squeezing the plastic mounting tabs together, and pulling outward and downward. (Figure DD-7.)

Now, using the special tool, remove the spanner nut from the centerpost. (Figure DD-8) If you need to tap on the spanner to remove the nut, be careful not to hit the porcelain interior of the basket. It will chip.

On the outside of the basket near the top, there will be a fill hole which is plugged up. If the hole is leaking, the basket must be replaced. The balancing ballast compartment cannot be serviced.

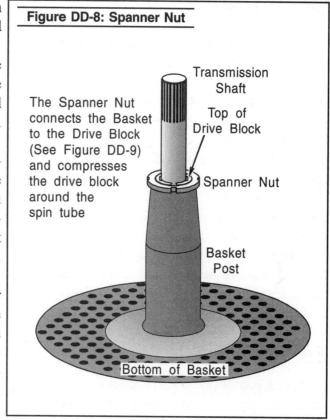

Figure DD-8: Spanner Nut

The Spanner Nut connects the Basket to the Drive Block (See Figure DD-9) and compresses the drive block around the spin tube

Transmission Shaft

Top of Drive Block

Spanner Nut

Basket Post

Bottom of Basket

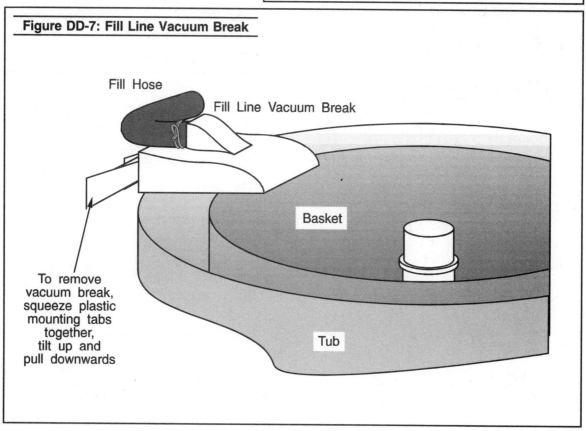

Figure DD-7: Fill Line Vacuum Break

Fill Hose

Fill Line Vacuum Break

Basket

To remove vacuum break, squeeze plastic mounting tabs together, tilt up and pull downwards

Tub

4-7 REMOVING THE TUB

Remove the agitator and basket as described in sections 4-5 and 4-6.

Remove the drive block by tapping upwards on the underside of it with a hammer. (Figure DD-9)

CAUTION: *the metal of the drive block is soft, so don't tap too hard, or you may damage it.*

Remove the water level switch hose and the tub drain hose from the tub. Have a bucket standing by to catch any leftover water in the drain hose.

Disconnect the pump hose and water level pressure switch hose from the tub. Some water may come out, so be prepared.

Remove the three suspension springs from the tub suspension brackets (figure DD-10) There will be a fourth, counterweight spring attached to either the left front bracket or the center rear bracket. Remove it.

CAUTION: *Mark all brackets and springs to be sure you get them back on the washer in exactly the same place.*

Remove the brackets from the tub.

Scrape any soap deposits off the centerpost, and lubricate it with some liquid soap so the tub will slide off easily. Pull the tub straight up and off the centerpost.

To replace the centerpost seal, squeeze it from inside the tub and push it through the bottom of the tub to the outside.

Re-assembly is the opposite of disassembly. Make sure all springs and brackets are in their original places. If any springs are broken, replace all *four* as a set.

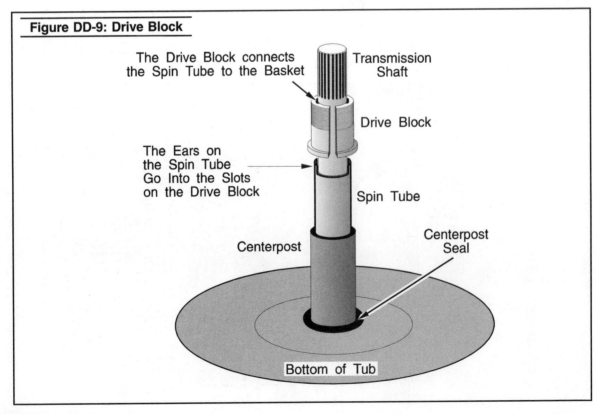

Figure DD-9: Drive Block

The Drive Block connects the Spin Tube to the Basket

Transmission Shaft

Drive Block

The Ears on the Spin Tube Go Into the Slots on the Drive Block

Spin Tube

Centerpost

Centerpost Seal

Bottom of Tub

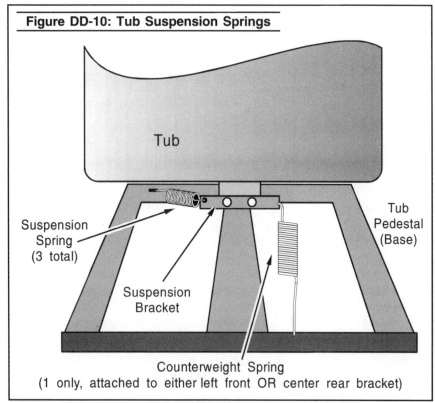

Figure DD-10: Tub Suspension Springs

Tub

Suspension
Spring
(3 total)

Suspension
Bracket

Tub
Pedestal
(Base)

Counterweight Spring
(1 only, attached to either left front OR center rear bracket)

4-8 MOTOR AND COUPLING

These machines have an external motor starting capacitor located in the console, not anywhere near the motor. To find it, open the console as de-scribed in section 4-2 and look inside the left side of the console. Before handling the motor, you must discharge and test the capacitor as described in section 2-6(e).

The motor coupling will break if the transmission locks up while the machine is running. It simply presses on to both the motor and transmission shafts. (Figure DD-11)

Do make sure the machine is unplugged before removing the motor.

If the motor is humming but not turning, remove it from the transmission as follows: (Figure DD-11.)

Disconnect power and remove the cabinet. (Section 4-2)

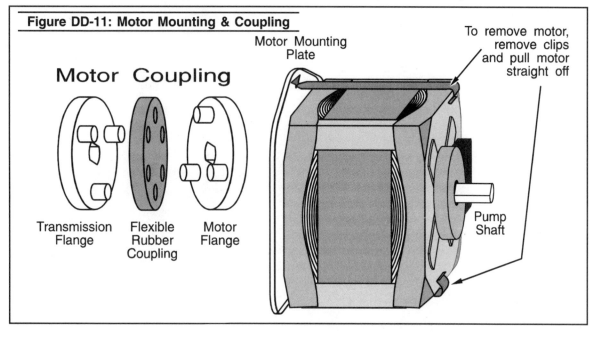

Figure DD-11: Motor Mounting & Coupling

Motor Mounting
Plate

To remove motor,
remove clips
and pull motor
straight off

Motor Coupling

Transmission
Flange

Flexible
Rubber
Coupling

Motor
Flange

Pump
Shaft

Following the safety precautions in section 1-4(4), lay the washer on its back and remove the two screws holding the bottom panel in place. Remove the bottom panel.

Remove the two spring clips holding the pump to the motor. No need to remove the pump hoses; just slide the pump off the motor shaft.

There may be two motor harness connectors, or only one. Disconnect it (them).

Two spring clips hold the motor to the transmission. (Figure DD-11) There may be screws holding the spring clips on; these are put on for shipping, and need not be re-installed. Remove the spring clips, and the motor will slide off.

Try turning the transmission by hand, in both directions. If it will not turn, it is locked up. Replace it as described in section 4-9. If

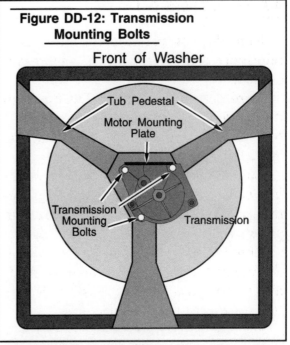

Figure DD-12: Transmission Mounting Bolts

it does turn easily, then either the starting switch or motor is bad. Test and repair as described in section 2-6(e).

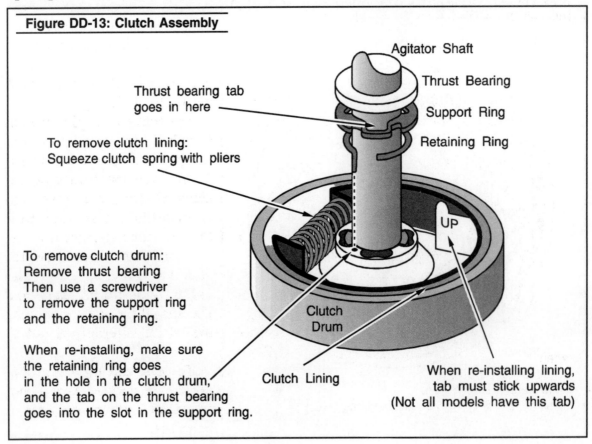

Figure DD-13: Clutch Assembly

Thrust bearing tab goes in here

To remove clutch lining: Squeeze clutch spring with pliers

To remove clutch drum: Remove thrust bearing Then use a screwdriver to remove the support ring and the retaining ring.

When re-installing, make sure the retaining ring goes in the hole in the clutch drum, and the tab on the thrust bearing goes into the slot in the support ring.

Agitator Shaft
Thrust Bearing
Support Ring
Retaining Ring

UP

Clutch Drum

Clutch Lining

When re-installing lining, tab must stick upwards (Not all models have this tab)

4-9 TRANSMISSION

Removal of the transmission is a relatively simple matter in these machines.

Remove the agitator, basket and drive block. (Section 4-5, 4-6 & 4-7) No need to remove the tub; just the drive block.

Lay the washer on its back and remove the two screws holding the bottom panel in place. Remove the bottom panel.

Remove the two spring clips holding the pump to the motor. No need to remove the pump hoses; just slide the pump off the motor shaft.

There may be two motor wiring harness connectors, or only one. Disconnect it (or them).

Remove the three transmission mounting bolts (Figure DD-12) and slowly pull the transmission straight out.

Installation is the opposite of removal. Make sure the brake tab is not in the way of the clutch spring. (See figure DD-14) Also be sure the motor coupling sticks out in the same direction as it did when you pulled the tranny off.

4-10 CLUTCH AND BRAKE

To service the clutch or brake, you must remove the transmission as described in section 4-9.

When you have removed the transmission, look on top of it for the clutch drum. (Figure DD-13) The clutch shoes can be removed simply by squeezing the spring with a pair of pliers. Check for a broken clutch spring or a worn clutch lining.

The brake and spin tube assembly is still attached to the tub pedestal. (Figure DD-14) To remove the spin tube assembly, turn the release cam counterclockwise and pull the spin tube straight out.

Inspect the spin tube for scoring. Also inspect the brake spring for breakage and the shoes for wear. Replace the whole assembly if defective.

To re-install the spin tube, go slowly and be careful not to catch or gouge any seals or bearings.

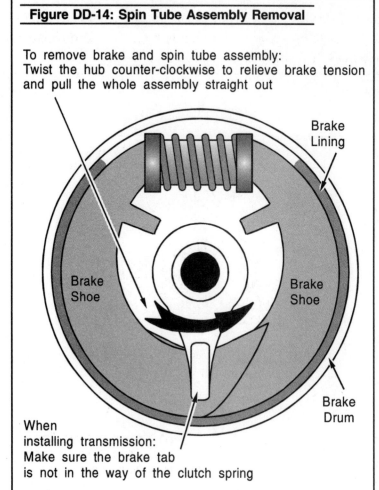

Figure DD-14: Spin Tube Assembly Removal

To remove brake and spin tube assembly:
Twist the hub counter-clockwise to relieve brake tension and pull the whole assembly straight out

Brake Lining

Brake Shoe

Brake Shoe

Brake Drum

When installing transmission:
Make sure the brake tab is not in the way of the clutch spring

4-11 TIMER

The timer can be removed by holding the timer dial while turning the timer knob to the left. The timer dial will then lift off a "D" shaped shaft, to reveal the timer mounting screws. (Figure DD-15.)

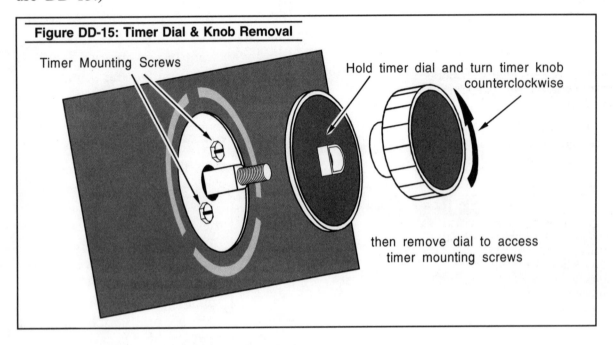

Figure DD-15: Timer Dial & Knob Removal

Timer Mounting Screws

Hold timer dial and turn timer knob counterclockwise

then remove dial to access timer mounting screws

Index

Also Available from EB Marketing Group
Brand-Specific Dryer & Top-Loading Washer Manuals!
for those who want a little LESS...
*Our brand-specific manuals have the same high quality instructions and illustrations
as our all-brand manuals, at a new low price!*

7th Edition

Whirlpool Dryer Repair
ISBN 1-890386-36-7   Part No. EBWD

7th Edition

Whirlpool Washer Repair
ISBN 1-890386-35-9   Part No. EBWW

*Whirlpool-brand manuals include
Kenmore, Kitchenaid, Estate
and Roper Brand Machines*

7th Edition

GE/Hotpoint Dryer Repair
ISBN 1-890386-38-3   Part No. EBGD

7th Edition

GE/Hotpoint Washer Repair
ISBN 1-890386-37-5   Part No. EBGW

*GE-brand manuals include
Hotpoint, late-model RCA, and
JC Penney (Penncrest) Brand Machines*

7th Edition

Maytag Dryer Repair
ISBN 1-890386-40-5   Part No. EBMD

7th Edition

Maytag Washer Repair
ISBN 1-890386-39-1   Part No. EBMW

Available from EB Marketing Group

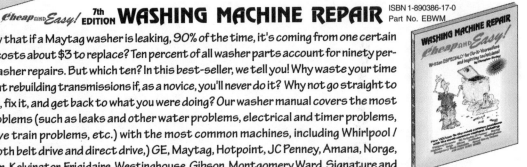